hank marvi
GUITAR TUTOR

"When I was a kid, all I wanted was a red electric guitar. It had to be red because of Hank and his magical sound. I never got that sound myself, but after years of trying to imitate other players I grew into my own style, as you will if you just keep playing and playing.

With the red imitation Stratocaster came a Shadows guitar book which taught me basic chords, even if it never taught me to play 'Wonderful Land' or 'Atlantis' the way Hank could. This tutor is a vast improvement on that old one, and it's a pleasure to preface it.

As the old salesman said to me as I was leaving the store with my first guitar - stick at it!

P.S. Hank still tells me that, too."

MARK KNOPFLER

Book designed by Headline Publicity Limited
Production by David Croft

First Published 1991
© International Music Publications

International Music Publications, Southend Road, Woodford Green, Essex IG8 8HN, England.

hank marvin's
GUITAR TUTOR
CONTENTS

INTRODUCTION

EQUIPMENT

What equipment do you use? is a question I've been asked many times. Well currently I play a Fender Stratocaster guitar through either a Mesa Boogie or Vox A.C. 30 amplifier and the only extra equipment I use is to get my sound is a Roland 301 Chorus Echo and a Morley volume pedal.

"I want to learn to play electric guitar, what should I buy and what amplifier and pedals need I get?" That's one I've heard a few times.

WHAT GUITAR?

For a beginner all you need is a lower priced though playable instrument. A guitar that I can recommend for the student is the Fender Squier Stratocaster which is excellent value for the money. I wish the Squier range of guitars had been around when I started.

WHAT AMPLIFIER?

Unless your intention is to destroy the hearing of your family and yourself there is no point in spending money on a big powerful amp to practice on. Buy a small practice amp and even if later you start playing with other musicians, maybe in a band, and want a bigger amp, a practice amp always comes in useful.

Apart from a guitar and amplifier all you really need at this stage is a lead to connect the instrument to the amp, a pick or plectrum and maybe an electronic tuner would be nice too. Later on you may want to add some sound processors like an echo or chorus, but right now you can get along well without them.

Well let's get stuck into playing some guitar shall we, as this course is aimed at beginners I advise you to start at the beginning and work through the tutor in order, not skipping any of the instructions.

Note, for each tune there are two backing tracks, the first one with the lead guitar and the second one without. This is so as you're learning a tune you can play along with my lead guitar on the first, then when you feel ready for it you can play along with the second one where you alone are the lead guitarist.

Remember to play every day and reap the benefits.

PLECTRUMS OR PICKS

As we are going to concentrate on playing the guitar plectrum style, let's spend a minute or two discussing picks or plectrums (by the way both terms can be used). Years ago they were usually made of tortoiseshell until the tortoises formed a union and told us to get off their backs, now composite plastic seems to be the more commonly used material. Plectrums like people, come in different shapes and sizes and some are thicker than others. Bruce Welch of the Shadows for example prefers a thin flexible plectrum for his distinctive rhythm style, while Brian May of Queen likes the stiffness of an old sixpenny piece! I prefer a new fifty pound note but usually make do with a medium thick plectrum of this shape and size. (1). More recently I have been using a smaller, very stiff pick which seems to give more control when fast picking. (2).

(1)   (2)

I suggest you start learning with the medium type, you can always experiment with different picks later.

HOLDING THE PLECTRUM

Hold the pick fairly firmly between the thumb and first finger of the right hand (see photos), but not so tight that you make your wrist and fingers tense up. That's uncomfortable and will make your arm ache.

MAKING A SOUND

Pick up your guitar and using your plectrum, pluck a string near the bridge. How does it sound? Thin, hard, metallic? Now pluck the string near the finger board, notice the change to a fuller softer, mellow tone. These tone colours can be used effectively in guitar playing but generally you'll find that a good tone is produced by picking the strings nearer the finger board than the bridge. When picking, keep a nice flexible wrist, making sure that the thumb and finger holding the pick are not allowed to flex and move around as you pick the notes. Keep them rigid and let the wrist do the work.

HOW TO HOLD THE GUITAR

It is a little easier to play the guitar while sitting down so you might want to start off that way. The instrument can be rested on either your right or left thigh, whichever feels most comfortable. You may find as I do that it's better to elevate the leg which is supporting the guitar by placing your foot on a classical guitarist's foot rest, a block of wood or the dog.

If you want to stand up and play, you'll need a nice pair of legs plus a guitar strap which goes over your left shoulder, is attached to the instrument and supports its weight. One advantage of standing up when playing is that if your audience turns hostile you can get off the stage that bit quicker.

It is important to make sure that you adjust the strap so that the guitar is supported at a comfortable height for easy playing. Try not to be influenced by photos of guitarists who have their guitars slung almost to their knees. It's very difficult, particularly for beginners, to play well with the guitar that low. So do yourself a favour, have it at a height that will help you play more easily. Why give yourself problems?

LEFT HAND

We finger the strings of the guitar with the left hand as follows: place the thumb in the centre of the back of the neck of the guitar and arch your fingers so that the finger tips can press down on the strings just behind the frets to produce the notes. You must press the string with a firm pressure in order to produce a clean note and a good tone. If insufficient pressure is applied then the strings tend to rattle. This can also be caused by long finger nails so it's best to keep the nails of your left hand cut short, sorry girls. It is important to make sure that the weight of the guitar is supported by your thigh when sitting and the strap when standing. Your left hand should not support any of the weight, otherwise your playing will be hindered.

In this photograph of the left hand position, note the thumb in the centre of the back of the guitar neck, with fingers arched pressing the strings firmly.

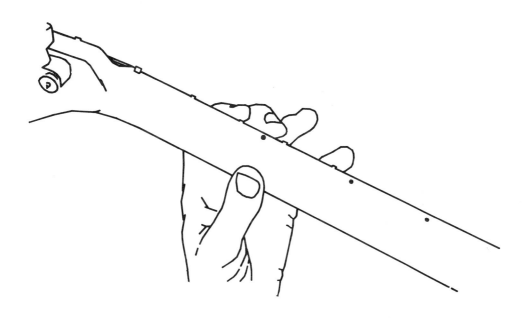

RIGHT HAND

As discussed on page one this is the hand that holds and manipulates the plectrum, using both up and down strokes from a flexible, slightly arched wrist. You may find as I do that when playing single string runs and melodies that it's a help to rest your little finger on the pick guard which can steady your hand and make picking more accurate. When strumming chords, as in playing a rhythm part, you may find it easier to let your fingers curl up naturally into a loose "fist" as you strum.

There are two signs used in connection with the right hand, this sign means a down stroke. ⊓ This one means an upstroke. V.

Most lead guitar played on single strings is done using alternate up and down strokes.

TUNING YOUR GUITAR

Not many people know that musical instruments played out of tune can have a detrimental affect on the environment, depleting the ozone layer and adversly affecting the breeding habits of certain wildlife, e.g. the Dodo! Of course this is not proven but we can never be too careful so always make sure your guitar is in tune. Funnily enough it sounds better as well.

Now let's consider some different ways of getting guitars in tune.

ELECTRONIC TUNERS

The easiest (and most accurate) way to tune a guitar is with the aid of an electronic tuner and this is how most professional and semi-pro guitarists tune their instruments. There are several different makes available and some are quite cheap so if you can afford to buy one of these I would recommend it, they are the best.

PITCH PIPES

These are also fairly easy to use, just tune each string to its individual note shown on the pitch pipe but one octave lower. If you try to tune the strings up to the pipe octave they'll probably break!

TO A PIANO

When you hold the guitar in the playing position, the string nearest you is the 6th or low E string which is the thickest and heaviest on the guitar. If you want to tune to a piano use the diagram below and find and play the note on the piano which corresponds to your 6th string, that is the second E below middle C. Pick the 6th string and by using the machine head (tuning peg) adjust the pitch of the string until it sounds in tune with the piano. Follow the same procedure with the other strings. By the way the guitar strings are tuned open not fretted.

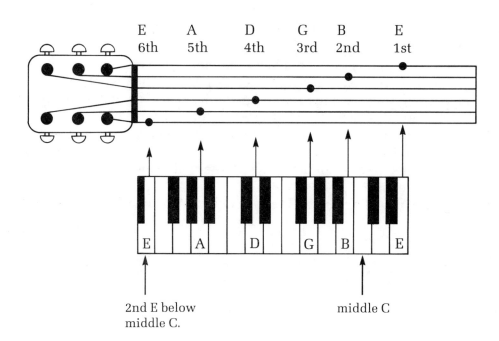

AN "A" TUNING FORK

This sounds a lot more complicated than it really is but it may prove useful.

The "A" tuning fork when struck, sounds the note of A which is the same note that the first (high E) string should produce if pressed down at the fifth fret. Here is the procedure step by step.

1) Tune the high E string so that when played at the fifth fret it sounds the same note as the fork. If it sounds higher than the fork, lower the pitch of string by turning the tuning peg, if lower raise the string by the same means.

2) With the second finger of the left hand press down the second string (B) just behind the fifth fret and with the right hand adjust the tuning peg to tune the string until it sounds the same note as the open (unfretted) first string (E).

3) With the first finger press down the third string (G) just behind the fourth fret and as before tune it until it sounds the same note as does the second string when played open.

4) With the second finger press down the fourth string (D) just behind the fifth fret and as before tune it until it sounds the same note as does the third string when played open.

5) Repeat the procedure on the fifth string (A) to tune to open fourth.

6) Repeat the procedure on the sixth string (E) to tune to open fifth.

STRINGS

As you've guessed already guitars sound nothing without strings. Fortunately there is a good choice of different makes of guitar strings available to us. These are manufactured in a variety of gauges or thicknesses or in some cases thinnesses. Basically they come in Heavy, Medium or Light gauge but there are variations on those main three, e.g. Extra light, Super light etc. The question is, **WHAT GAUGE SHOULD YOU USE?** I expect that you'll want to be able to bend notes when you play so you'll really need LIGHT GAUGE strings. (The thinner they are the easier they bend.) If too thin though they don't have such a good tone and also go out of tune more easily. I recommend the following:

Strings	1st	2nd	3rd	4th	5th	6th
Gauge	010	013	017	028	038	048 or 050

These are the gauges I use most of the time but if you want something even lighter and easier to bend on the lower strings then try this.

1	2	3	4	5	6
010	013	016	026	036	046

Notice the lighter gauges on the 3rd, 4th, 5th and 6th strings used by many guitarists. Any friendly neighbourhood guitar shop should either stock or be able to get you strings of these gauges.

LET'S PLAY A TUNE

When I got my first guitar I just couldn't wait to start playing single note melody lines and solos. Is that how you feel? Well I'd be surprised if it isn't, so let's go ahead and play some tunes.

Now to play single note melodies you really have to know where to put your fingers in order to produce the notes, so on the following pages we'll take a look at some notes on all six strings and then use them to play tunes. To help you learn the notes and fingering for these tunes we'll be using some diagrams.

In this book the diagrams will have the **horizontal lines as strings** and the **vertical lines as frets**.

The first type of diagram we will be using is one in which both notes and fingering are indicated. This is symbolised by the following.

A circle with a letter inside indicates the note produced by fretting the string.

The number alongside the circle indicates the finger of the left hand to be used

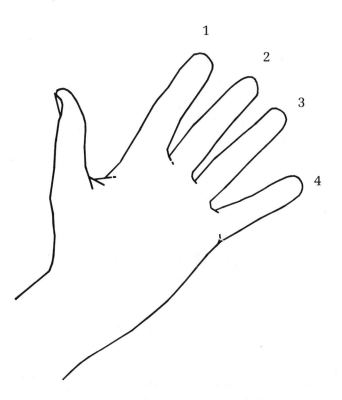

Remember, the left hand fingers are numbered like this.

In case you wish to refer to it there is at the back of the book a section on the basic rudiments of music which you will find helpful.

If you're ready turn over the page and get started with the notes on the first string.

THE NOTES ON THE FIRST STRING (E)

We will learn four notes on the first string

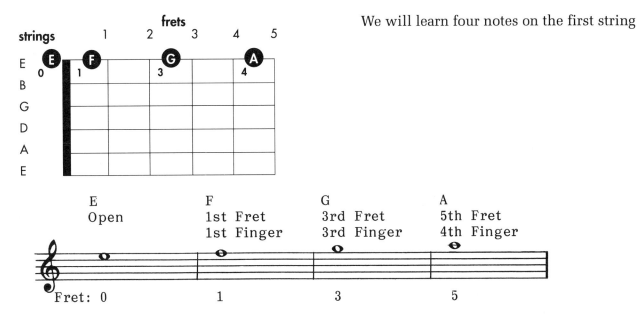

Although ultimately we are aiming for a good right hand technique using alternate up and down strokes we will for the moment use down strokes only (⊓) for the following exercises.

We start with WHOLE NOTES (Or Semibreves) and a WHOLE NOTE (o) receives FOUR BEATS.
Strike the string on the first beat and hold the note on for the remaining three.

Now HALF NOTES (Or Minim), each HALF NOTE (♩) receives TWO BEATS

And QUARTER NOTES (or Crotchets), a QUARTER NOTE (♩) receives ONE BEAT.

THE NOTES ON THE SECOND STRING (B)

Three notes on the 2nd string

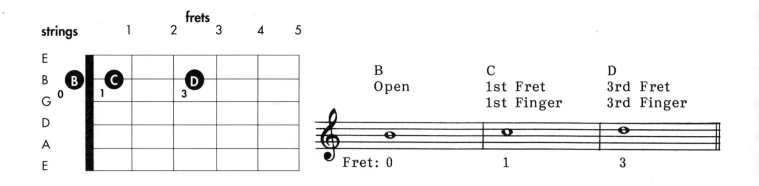

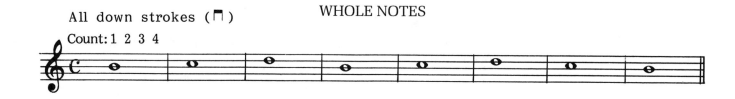

All down strokes (⊓)

WHOLE NOTES

HALF NOTES

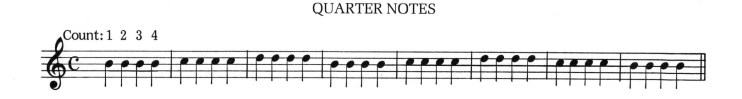

QUARTER NOTES

Now let's play a tune on the E and B strings using the notes and fingerings you have learned. I'll play it for you on the cassette so you can hear how it should go but when you listen follow along reading the music.

THE FIRST TWO

Hank Marvin

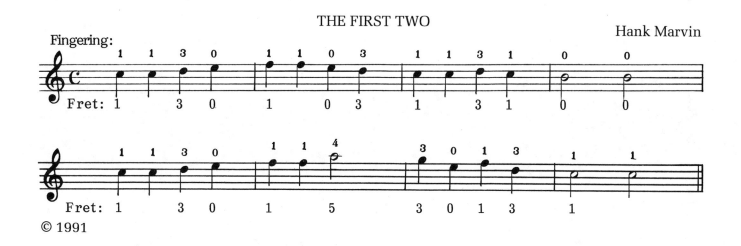

© 1991

Only two notes on the third string.

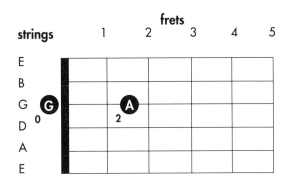

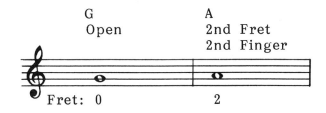

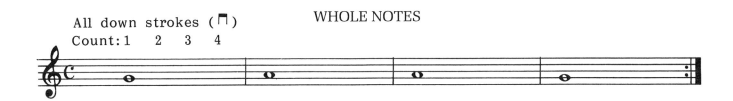

All down strokes (⊓)
Count: 1   2   3   4

WHOLE NOTES

HALF NOTES

Count: 1   2   3   4

QUARTER NOTES

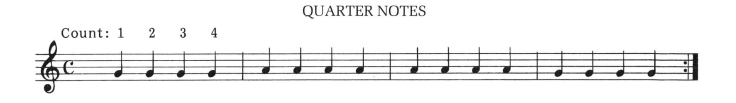

Count: 1   2   3   4

You have now learned (unless you've been slacking) the first position notes on the E or 1st; The B or 2nd; and the G or 3rd strings. Here's how they all look together to remind you of the correct fingering and fret number to use.

THE NOTES ON THE E-1st, B-2nd, and G-3rd

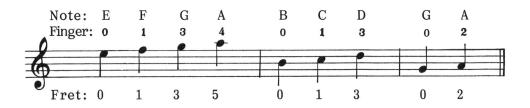

Just before we get onto the solos I'd like to introduce you to something that will make things easier for you. It's called **TABLATURE**: an example of which is below.

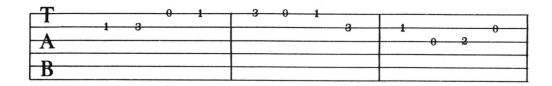

Tablature has six lines representing the six guitar strings. The numbers on the lines (or strings) indicate the fret at which the string is to be pressed down. The correct fingering will be shown on the music above.

Using only the 1st, 2nd and 3rd strings let's get down to the enjoyable business of playing solo guitar. Play these pieces **slowly at first** aiming for clean accurate notes, as your technique improves with practice so you're be able to play faster.

Continue to pick using **all down strokes** with the thumb and finger holding the pick held rigid, the wrist providing the down stroke.

Now listen to the cassette while following along with the music.

ONE TWO THREE

An exercise.

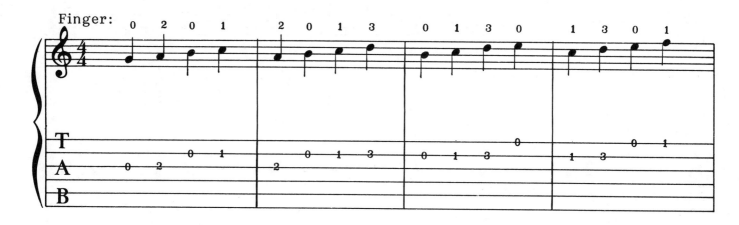

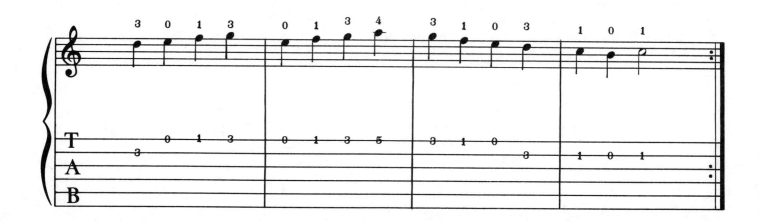

Now over the page are two tunes that you can learn to play, an old one and a new one. Both can be played along with the backing tracks which are on the cassette.

YANKEE DOODLE

The repeat sign (: ▌) at the last bar directs us to play the piece thru' twice.

Traditional

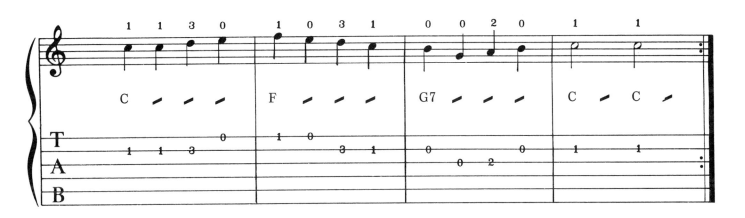

M A R I K O

Hank Marvin

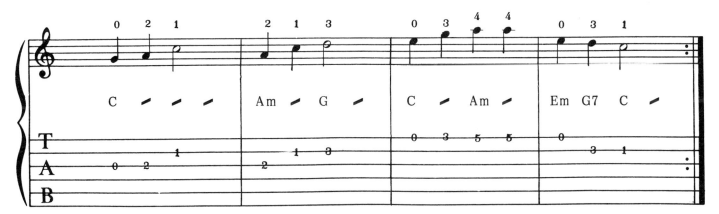

© 1991

* The chord charts have been included so that later you can use them to practise the chords you will be learning.

THE NOTES ON THE FOURTH STRING (D)

Three notes on the 4th string.

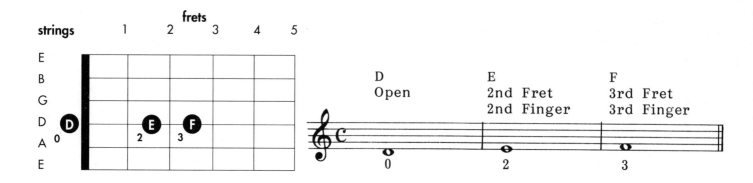

WHOLE NOTES

HALF NOTES

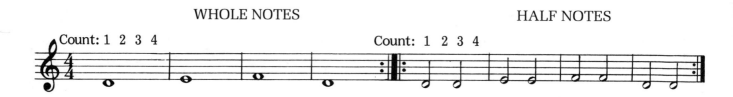

QUARTER NOTES

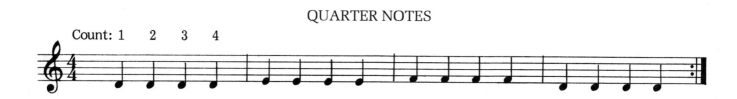

Here's a little solo using the first four strings. Check it with the cassette.

FOUR ON THE FLOOR

Hank Marvin

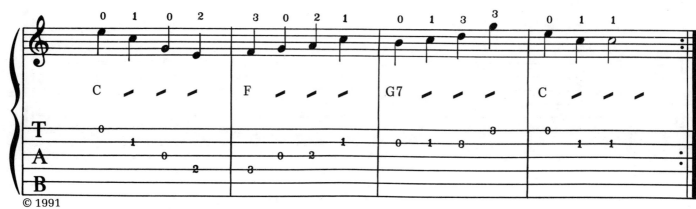

© 1991

Three notes on the 5th string

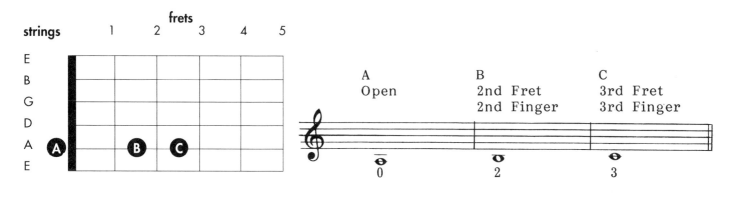

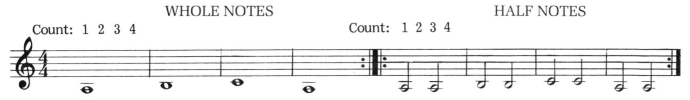

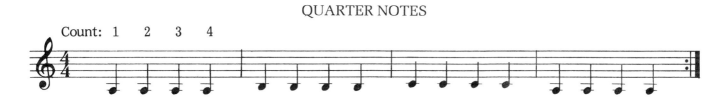

Here's a little eight bar tune written especially for the fingering you've learned on the 3rd, 4th and 5th strings. Listen to the cassette.

TREMILLE

Hank Marvin

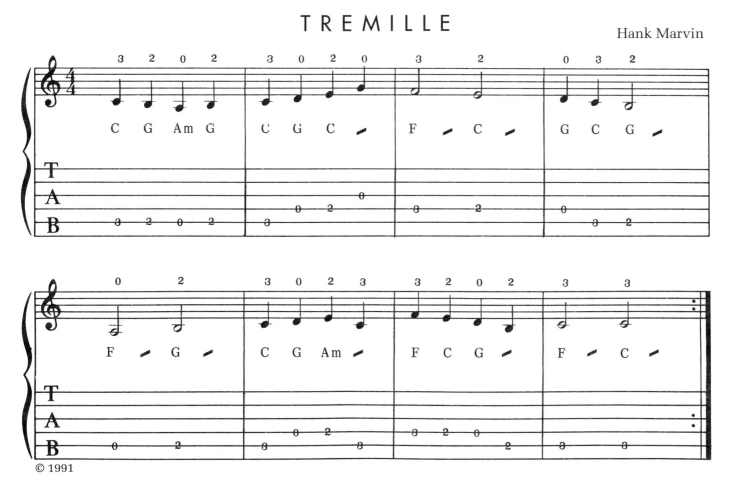

© 1991

Three notes on the 6th string

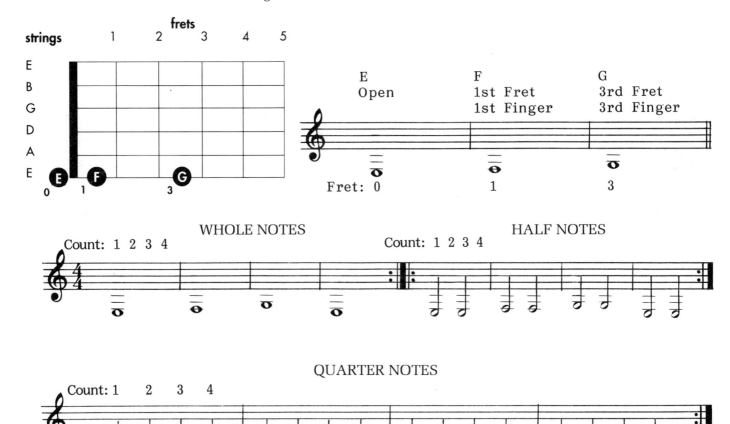

Here's a low down piece on the 5th and 6th strings that you can really dig into using all down strokes of the pick. Check it out with the cassette.

RACE WITH THE BASS

Hank Marvin

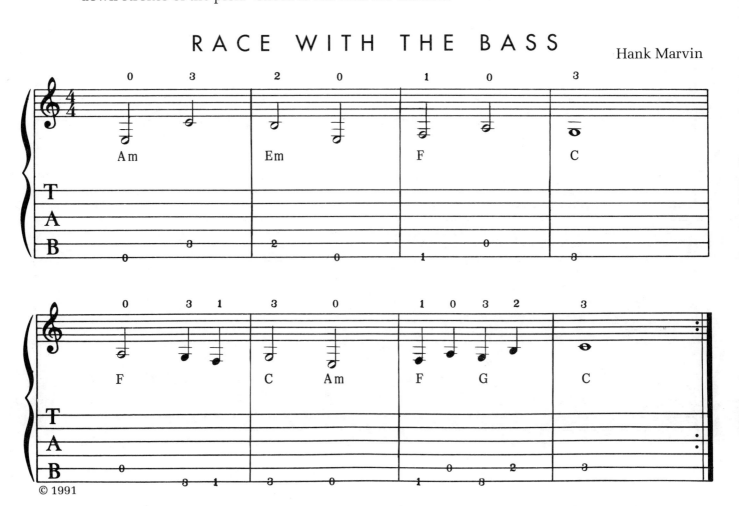

Here's a reminder of those first position notes with the fret numbers and correct fingering. Remember the **fret and finger numbers** are with one exception **exactly the same**. The **exception** is on the **1st string** where we have **the A** played on the **5th fret** with the **4th finger**.

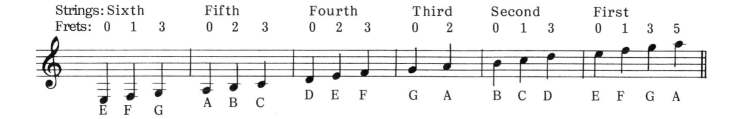

ALTERNATE PICKING

Now it's time to further your picking technique so instead of using all down strokes with the pick, you'll now start to use alternate up and down strokes. This is called alternate picking and is how we pick most of the time. Below is an exercise to help you develop this. As you play it, start the first note with a down stroke and play the next with an upstroke and so on alternatively picking down up down up. Remember to keep the finger and thumb holding the pick rigid letting the wrist provide the movement.

Follow along with the cassette.

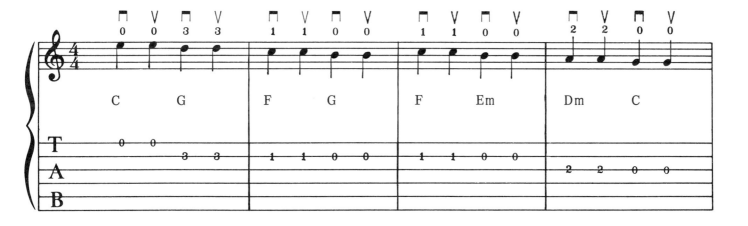

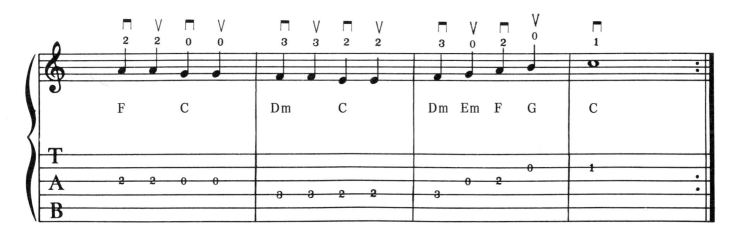

Now go back to page ten and work through all the previous pieces using alternate picking and when you feel comfortable with the technique we can move on over the page to a tune that covers all the notes you've learned on all six strings.

SIX OF THE BEST

As mentioned on the previous page this next piece contains all the notes that we have so far learned and these are from the first position C scale, of which a detailed explanation is given on page 17. As before work along with the cassette and use all six strings with alternative picking to dish out six of the best.

SIX OF THE BEST

Hank Marvin

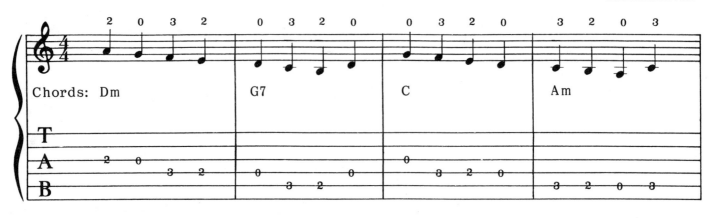

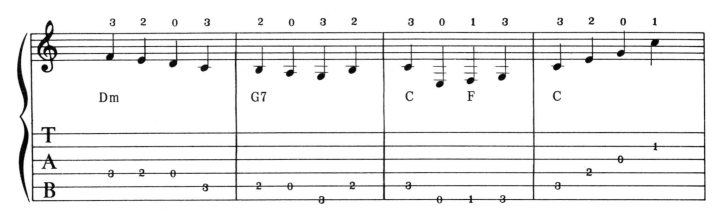

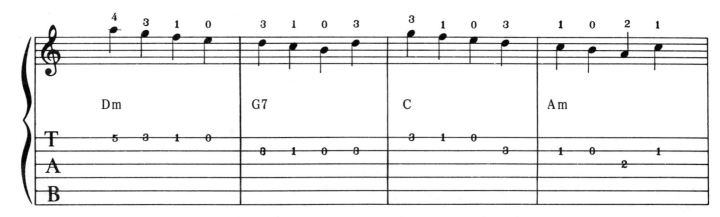

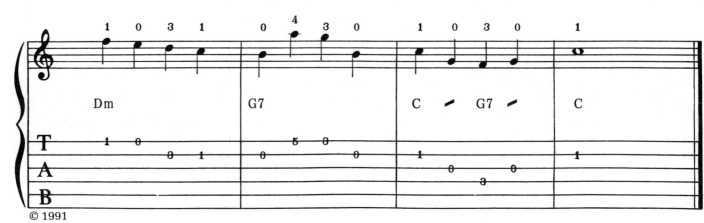

THE KEY OF C

The music we've been playing so far using the first position notes has been in the Key of C. That means that the notes have been taken from the C Major Scale. We call it that because the first note of this scale is a C.

So, we start the C scale on the note of C and then go through the musical alphabet until C appears again, like this **C--D--E--F--G--A--B--C**

THE C SCALE

ascending   descending

STEPS

The distance from one tone to the next higher or lower tone is called a HALF-STEP which on the guitar is ONE FRET.

e.g. The C scale has two Half steps and they are between E-F and B-C. A WHOLE STEP is made up of TWO HALF STEPS. So the distance of a WHOLE STEP on the guitar is TWO FRETS.

e.g. C-D, D-E, F-G, G-A, and A-B are Whole steps.

Although Whole steps and Half steps are also referred to as Whole tones and Half tones, I prefer to use "steps" as it suggests moving up or down the scale.

RELATIVE MINOR

Each Major Key has a Relative Minor Key which is built upon the Sixth Tone of the Major Scale. The Relative Minor of C Major is A minor.

The first note of the A Minor Scale is of course A (which is the sixth tone of the C Scale).

We start on A and work our way through the musical alphabet until we meet A again, like this. **A--B--C--D--E--F--G--A**.

Although the minor scale has three forms: 1. NATURAL or PURE; 2. HARMONIC; 3. MELODIC, we will for the moment consider only the first one, the Natural.

THE A MINOR SCALE

(Natural)

The position of Whole and Half steps in the minor scale is different. The **Half steps** in the **Natural Minor** are between the **2nd and 3rd** and the **5th and 6th** notes. (In the Major between 3rd and 4th & 7th and 8th).

RACE WITH THE BASS

We played eight bars of this earlier in the book but now let's learn the whole piece taking it one section at a time and then putting it all together. I'll go through this with you on the cassette.

THE INTRO

This is four bars in length but as there is a WHOLE NOTE REST (⬛) which **means four beats rest**, you play nothing in the first bar.
You do however have a two bar phrase to play over bars two and three, but look at the first beat of bar two, there you'll see a QUARTER NOTE REST (𝄽) which means that you play nothing for that **one beat**. The fourth bar like the first, is a one bar rest.

THE VERSE

The verse which is sixteen bars long and played on the 5th and 6th strings is made up of half notes (count two beats per note), and some quarter notes (one beat per note).

THE MIDDLE

The middle is eight bars in length and is played on the first four strings. Look out for the first beat of bars one and five because there you have a quarter note rest which means that you play nothing for that one beat of the bar. At the end of the middle you find a REPEAT SIGN (:𝄁) **so go back to the beginning** where you'll find the other sign and **play through from there again**.
When you get to the end of the last bar of the verse, bar sixteen, you will see a sign telling you to go TO ⨁ CODA. Well don't just stand there, do it, go from there **straight to the sign that says CODA ⨁** and play the four bars of the CODA to finish.

THE CODA

The Coda is actually a drawn out version of the last two bars of the verse: same melody notes but played longer with half notes instead of quarter notes. The last two bars of the Coda have two notes of the same pitch (C) tied together with a curved line. That means that they are TIED NOTES and therefore are **played as just one long note instead of two separate ones**. So play the first C and let it sustain or ring on over into that last bar.

This is **all first position fingering as in the previous pieces,** but don't be afraid to refer back if you feel the need. OK, let's go through this together with the cassette.

RACE WITH THE BASS

Hank Marvin

MIDDLE

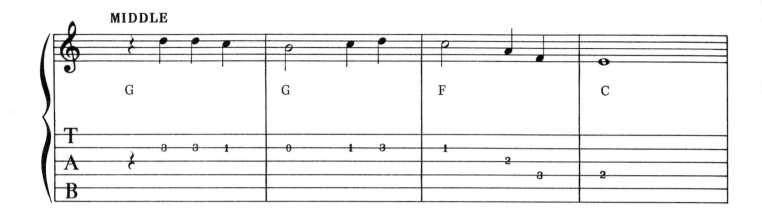

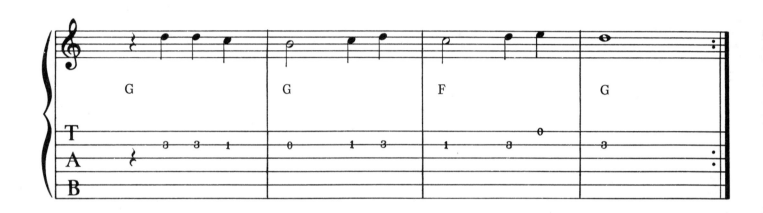

CODA

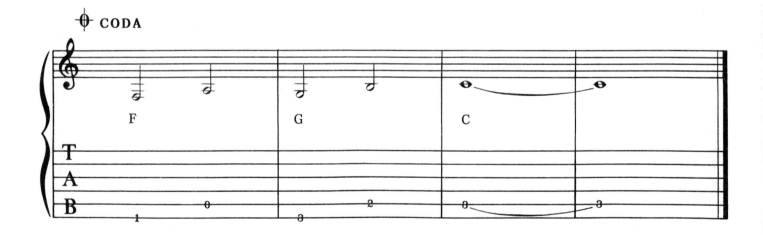

As mentioned on page eleven the chord sequences to all these little tunes were included so you could use them to practise when you learned those chords. Well the time is now! So turn over the page and get started on your first chords.

Up until now we've been concentrating on just playing single note melodies, but there is another aspect of guitar playing that we should consider and that is chord playing. Although mainly used for rhythm accompaniment, chord playing can also be employed effectively in guitar solos. (Listen to the guitar solo on Buddy Holly's "Peggy Sue" for example).

A chord is a combination of several notes played together, which means you have to use more than one finger at once. Frightening isn't it? But you can do it.

Now at first you'll probably find your fingers incredibly reluctant to obey your commands, almost as if they belonged to someone else, but don't be disheartened because it happens to every beginner, in fact it still happens to me sometimes but keep that to yourself. If though you spend some time getting familiar with these chord shapes and practising them, you'll find that it gets easier and easier to place your fingers where you want them so that in a short time you'll be able to change from once chord to the other fairly smoothly (eventually **really** smoothly). The following diagrams are to show you where to place your left hand fingers in order to produce a chord. As with the previous diagrams **the horizontal lines represent the strings** and the **vertical lines the frets**.

The letters above the diagrams are **chord symbols** and tell us the name of the chord shown in the diagram.

The first two chords to learn are C major and G7. An 0 means that the string is played open. If it's not fingered or marked 0 do not play the string.

Learn the easier fingering first to get the feel of playing chords, then aim to learn the full fingered versions.

(easier version)

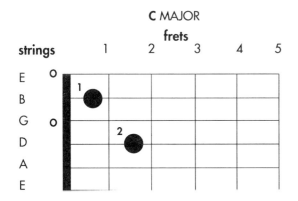
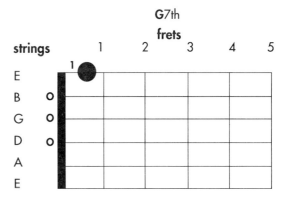

(full fingering)

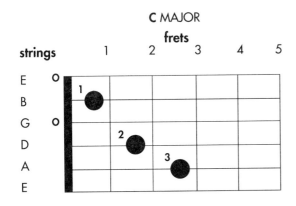
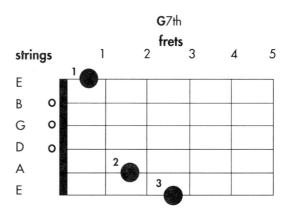

USING THE CHORDS

Are you ready for your fist chord sequence? Well here is a rhythm part using the C and G7 chords. On this first piece strum the chords not on every beat but only on the first and third beats, letting the chords ring through to the second and fourth beats.

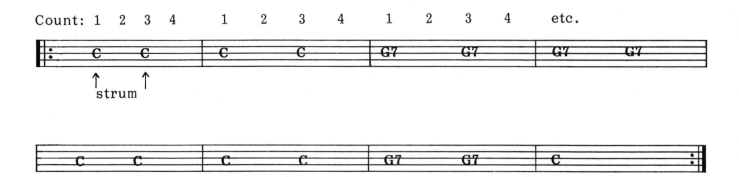

This sign (/) which is used in the chord chart below simply means continue playing the chord last indicated. Using the same two chords and the backing track on the cassette, we'll now play a famous old folk song together.

SKIP TO MY LOU

Traditional

Lost my partner   what'll I do lost my partner   what'll I do

Lost my partner what'll I do Skip to my lou my dar-ling -

Hey - Hey - Skip to my lou Hey - Hey - Skip to my lou

Hey - Hey - Skip to my lou - Skip to my lou my darling

Play along with the cassette as often as you like so as to get really confident with the chords, aiming for clean smooth changes from one to the other. Remember, always practise new things slowly, letting speed come naturally.

Here are two more chords to add to your repetoire, **A minor** and **D minor**.

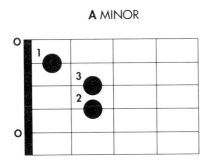

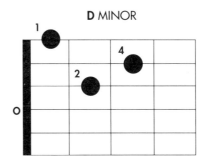

Familiarise yourself with the fingering and then practise changing from one chord to the other in the following exercise, slowly at first until you develop accurate finger placement.

Count: 1 2 3 4 etc.

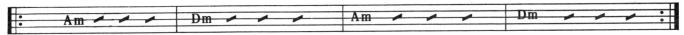

Now, using the four chords you've learned, C, Am, Dm, and G7, you can play the rhythm part for a lovely old song "Au Clair de La Lune".

Have a look at the chord chart below and you'll see that the chords change every two beats, which will keep you on your toes. It could be effective on this tune to play the chords only on the first beat of the changes, letting them sustain through the next beat. You may also want to vary it and try gently strumming instead. Get familiar with the changes first and then play along with the backing track on the cassette.

AU CLAIR DE LA LUNE

Traditional

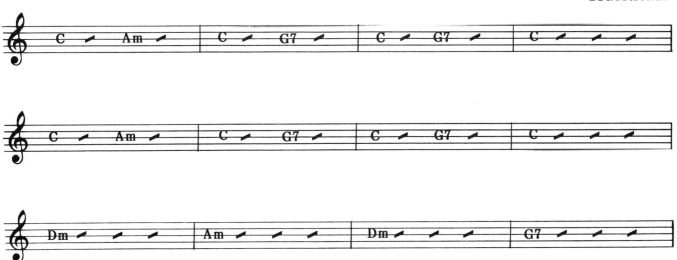

SWEET ROSE

Still using those same four chords we'll play another tune. Again, you may want to vary your approach to playing the rhythm part. This time try gently strumming up and down so that you're in effect strumming twice per beat, making it eight strums a bar. To help you, you could count it like this:

Normal count	One	Two	Three	Four
You count	One and	two and	three and	four and

The tune is also written out so you can learn to play that as well.

SWEET ROSE

Hank Marvin

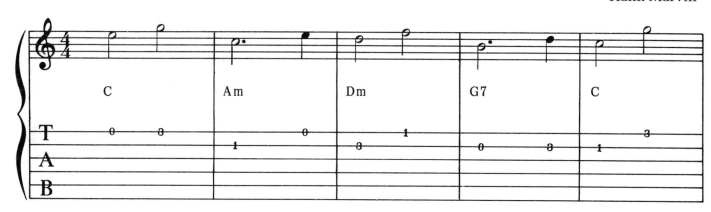

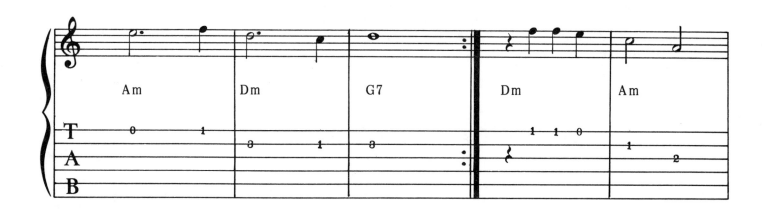

Note. Strum the first beat only of the last bar, allowing the chord to sustain through the last three beats.

A 12 Bar blues is so called because it is a sequence of chords, twelve bars in length and derived from the original blues sequence. There have been many many big rock n' roll and pop hits based on this format. eg. "The Rise And Fall Of Flingel Bunt" recorded by The Shadows.

To play a twelve bar blues in the key of C we need to learn two new chords. These are the chords of F and C7 and the diagrams are shown below.

Notice how this C7 chord shape is basically the same as the C shape you already know, with the addition of the fourth finger holding down the third string, 3rd fret.

For the F chord, your first finger must press down the 1st and 2nd strings at the same time. This is called a 'bar'. The top joint of the finger goes flat across the strings.

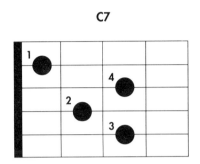
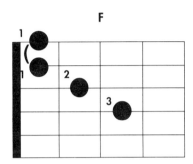

PRACTICE SLOWLY

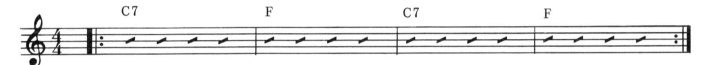

If you look at the following chord chart you'll notice that before the twelve bar sequence starts we have a little intro of two bars played over a G7 chord.

Dedicated it to all Scots guitarists this is called C U Jimmy Blues. So run it through a couple of times and then try it with the cassette.

"C. U. JIMMY" BLUES

You can also use this chord chart to play along with the up tempo rock'n'roll 12 bar on the cassette.

Another chord sequence that has been used in the writing of so many hit songs is the one we're about to play now. You know the chords already, it's in the key of C and I'm sure you'll recognise the sequence when you play it.

This is played with a slow Rock ballad feel and we'll have an intro of one bar of G7. So get the feel of the chord changes, have a listen to the cassette and then play along with me.

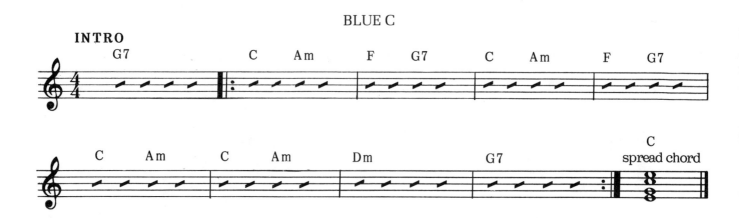

BLUE C

Well time to move right along now and learn some new chords:

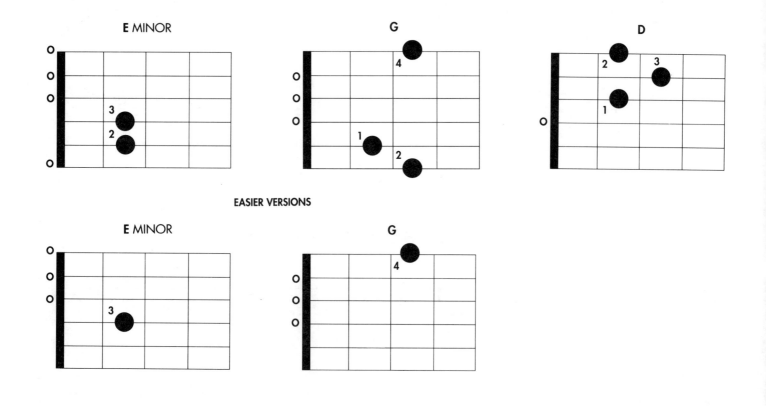

AN EXERCISE

Spend some time practising and remembering these new chords and we'll use them in the next piece of music.

Along with others we're going to use the last three chords you learned (Em, G and D) in this next sequence. It is in the key of G - yes we have the technology and it is a type of chord progression used to good effect by the Kinks and the Who among others.

Now for this tune instead of strumming just once on every beat, try strumming one down stroke and one upstroke per beat in an even eight feel. It may help you to count like this:

instead of this: 1   2   3   4   1   2   3   4

I'll demonstrate this for you on the tape. Have a listen, try the changes which are mainly every two beats and when you're ready play along with the track on the cassette.

REPEATER

Hank Marvin

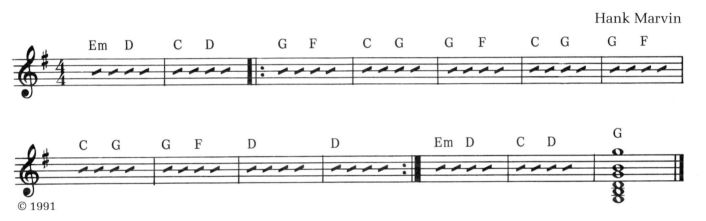

To broaden your experience of reading and playing chord charts it would be a good idea to go back and learn to play the rhythm parts of all the tunes you've played so far in the book, and remember, if you practise these chord changes regularly, you'll quickly get to the stage where your fingers will just grab the shapes with you having to think no more about it than you do when you're breathing. I'm assuming of course that you do breathe without too much thought!

I hope that you've enjoyed overcoming any difficulties in learning to play these chords because you will have not only improved your ability as a guitarist but will have increased the amount of pleasure you'll get from the instrument.

OK now we'll move on and turn our attention back to single note melody playing.

It's time now for a little "Rock'n'Roll", so let's look at what is possibly "The Great Rock'n Blues Riff" which no guitarist would be without. It will be played on the lower four strings (G, D, A and E) and to get the right sound we have to play two strings at a time! Sounds difficult but it's not and with a little practice and perseverance you'll soon master it.

Let's learn the riff in the key of A because we can use open strings which makes it easier to play.

It would be best to follow the Tablature and the fingering directions because being in the key of A, some notes (F, G and C) are played as sharp notes (F♯. G♯ and C♯). That means that the note is played one fret higher (a semitone) than the natural note.

In this riff it's only the top notes that change, so let's look at them first and until you get the hang of it play it slow. As it's written in EIGHTH NOTES count through each bar like this: **one** and **two** and **three** and **four** and.

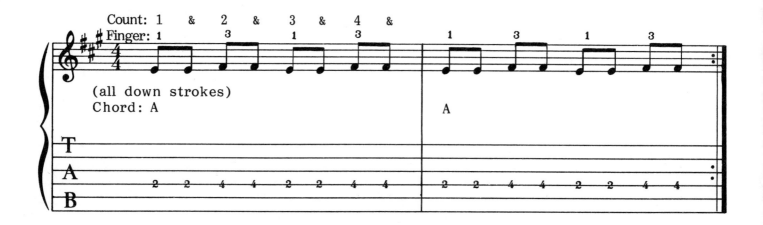

Now add the lower note which is simply the open A string by striking the D and A strings simultaneously sounding the two notes at the same time.

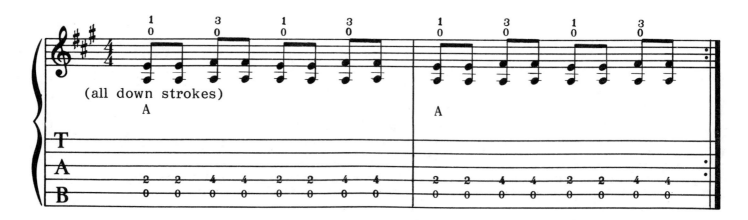

Now do **exactly** the same thing on the D and G strings using the same fingering and fretting, the moving line on the G string, the D played open.

Follow the procedure again on the Low E and A strings, moving line on the A string, E played open. The riff sounds better if you "damp" the strings by resting the heel of your right hand (not too heavily) on the bridge. Experiment with this by moving your hand until you get the right sound comparing it to the cassette.

The following chord sequence is a typical Rock or Blues 12 Bar. Use it along with the cassette to practise the Rock'n Blues riff and its following variations.

As these new chords will be taught a little later on please don't be concerned about playing them now. **Concentrate on playing the riff**.

The riff works over the chords like this: over the A chords use the A and D strings to play the riff; Over the D chords use the D and G strings, and over the E chords use the E and A strings as in the example below.

EXAMPLE

(Note the C♯)

12 BAR SEQUENCE IN THE KEY OF A

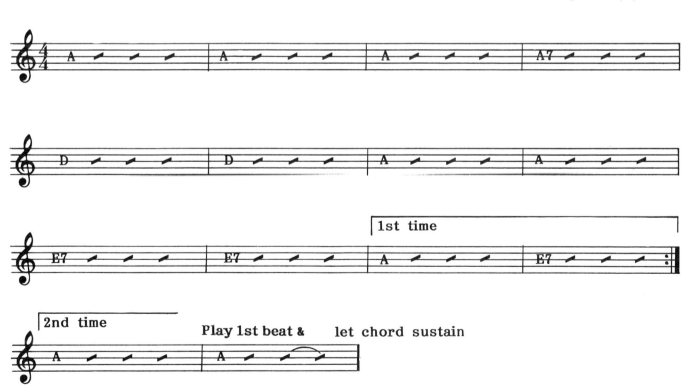

Over the page you'll find two examples of variations on the basic riff, look and see how they are different, learn them and then try them out with the 12 Bar and the cassette. Go for it.

VARIATIONS

A number of possible variations of this basic riff can be discovered by either:

1) A different combination of notes played on the highest of the two strings.
2) The use of different phrasing. Or 3) By combining 1 and 2.

OK so let's consider two variations achieved by the first method and to learn these we'll adopt the same procedure as with the basic riff you've just learned. Although played on two strings **only the moving line on the highest string will be shown** because the lower string stays on the one note and is played as before.

Note: In both variations the G is played as G natural (♮) not as a G♯. So take care to get the right fretting and fingering.

VARIATION (a)

VARIATION (b)

As with the basic riff these can be played on the D and G strings (Note: play C natural on the G string) and E and A strings, using exactly the same fretting and fingering as above. Try out these variations with the "12 Bar" backing track.

Before we go on to the next piece of music let's talk about Tied Notes, Dotted Notes and Slurs. What do they look like? What are they used for?

TIED NOTES

In a piece of music you will often see two or more notes of the same pitch "tied" together by a curved line like this (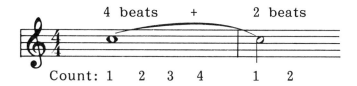) the note is played only once but lasts for the combined number of beats of the notes.

Pick the first note and let it ring for the total length of all the tied notes. This is often used to lengthen a note across a bar line as in the example.

DOTTED NOTES

A dot placed after a note increases the value or duration of that note by one half of it's original value. In other words the note would last half as long again.

2 beats + 1 beat = 3 beats

THE SLUR OR SLIDE

Slurring or sliding on the guitar is nothing to do with drinking too much, it simply means that we play a phrase of two or more different notes by picking only the first note and then sliding a finger on to the next notes in the phrase. This can be shown musically by tying the notes together with a line and adding an S (for slide).
e.g. / = upward slide, \ = downward slide.

* NOTE: This is not the same as "slide" guitar which is played with a steel or "bottle neck" and not fingers.

SLIDING AROUND IN A MINOR

In the first of these two pieces in A minor we use downward slides, and to accommodate the slides the fingering has been altered, so look out!
There is also a tied note in the 4th bar with the E starting on the 2nd beat.

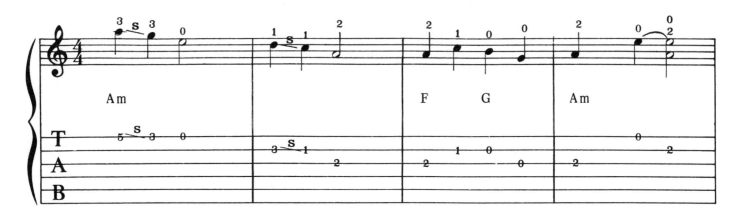

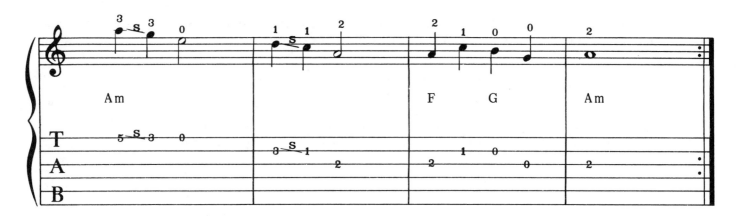

The second piece has both **upward and downward slides** and a twice occurring **dotted note**. Again look out for the fingering on the slides.

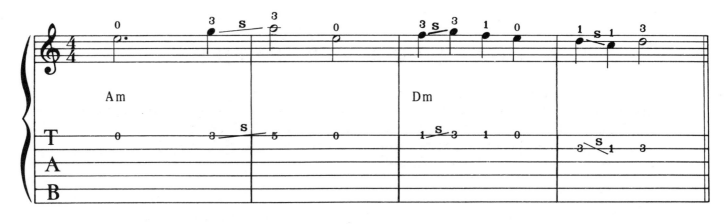

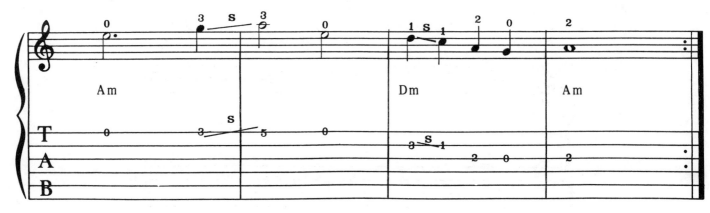

Check it out with the cassette.

M O R E   C H O R D S

The most popular keys for guitar are E, A, D, G and C, and by an amazing coincidence we happen to have here a little piece of music that moves through every one of those keys using the three basic chords in each of them. The tune is built on an eight bar sequence which is played in each of the above keys in turn before coming back to the original key of E.

Starting in the key of E first of all, learn the new chords and then practise the sequence in that key. When you feel confident with that you can then move on to the next key.

E
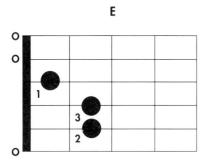

E7
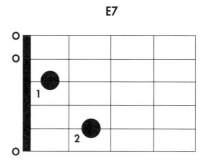

A
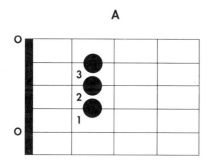

B7
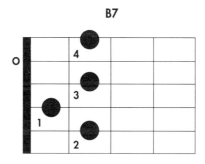

Count: 1 2 3 4   1 2 3 4   etc.

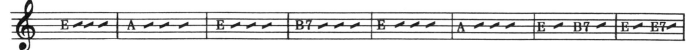

Now in the key of A follow the same procedure as above but this time before moving onto the next key, practice playing from the start in E right through to the end of the sequence in the key of A. When you feel happy with that you can move on to the next section.

A7
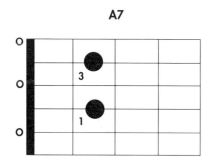

D
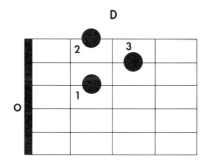

We move the Key of D now and after learning the chords and the changes, play from the beginning of the sequence in E through to the end of the sequence in D. Repeat this procedure with the remaining keys until you have learned the entire piece and then play along with the cassette.

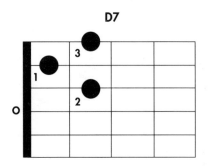

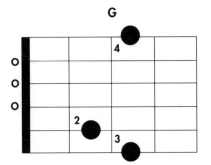

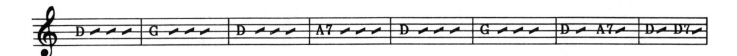

Now we have it in the key of G so learn it and add it to the previous sequences.

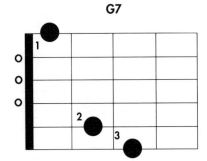

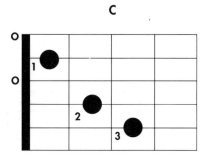

This is in the key of C, the last change before we come back to our starting key, **look out** for the **B7 chord** on the **last two beats** of the **eighth bar** which is there to lead us back into the key of E.

You should know all the chords for the last section and the sequence is as you can see, the same as the beginning except for the eighth bar which doesn't change to an E7 but stays on the E. The ending is just two beats on each chord apart from the last bar where you play the E on the first beat and let it ring through the bar. So practise this last section from bar ♯41 on the chord chart and then try the whole thing from the top with the cassette.

H E A D I N G   F O R   H O M E

Hank Marvin

Count: 1 2 3 4   1 2 3 4   etc.

Bar #41

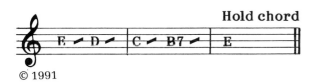

© 1991

SCALES: MAJOR AND MINOR

Whether playing tunes or improvising solos as in jazz or rock 'n' roll we are using scales of one kind or another (as you found out earlier with the tunes written on the C major and A minor scales), so it's important to get to know them.

A scale is a series of eight notes and it is the position of the whole steps (whole tones) and half steps (half tones) within that scale which determines whether it is major or minor.

MAJOR SCALE
Half steps occur between
3rd & 4th and 7th & 8th notes.

NATURAL MINOR SCALE
Half steps occur between
2nd & 3rd and 5th &6th notes

The note from which a scale starts is called the key note and the scale takes it's name from that note, as we saw with the C major scale starting on the note of C and the A minor scale starting on, (no prizes for this) the note of A.

We need various scales so that music can be written, played and sung in higher or lower keys, because a key that is good for one singer may be too high or low for another. In order to keep the whole steps and half steps in their correct positions within the scales, we use sharps and flats to raise or lower a note half a step, which on the guitar is one fret.

THE SHARP
This sign ♯ before a note
means that it is raised or
sharpened by one half step.

THE FLAT
This sign ♭ before a note
means that it is lowered or
flattened by one half step.

As you will soon see some keys have a lot of sharps or flats in them, so to avoid placing these signs before every note that requires it we use a key signature which shows us which notes have to be raised or lowered. The key signature for the key of G for example is one sharp.

Key of G

Notice that the sharp sign is on the F line which means that every F is sharpened or raised half a step (one fret). This applies not only to the F on the top line of the stave but to every F whatever its position on the stave or ledger lines. This can be cancelled only by the placing of a natural sign (♮) in front of any particular F. This natural sign applies to every F in that register for the duration of the bar in which it is used. We would then revert to the sharp F as in the key signature. Try the following example.

This example is in the Key of G so the key signature is one sharp (all F notes raised half a step) but look out for the second bar because we have a natural on the F line.

Sharps and flats placed before notes in the course of a piece of music and not marked at the beginning are termed accidentals and as we saw with the natural they are only effective in the bars in which they are found.

Having already looked at the **C major scale and it's relative minor (Am)** we'll move on to the other main guitar keys starting with **G major and it's relative minor (Em)**. The fret and finger numbers are identical on these two scales.

G M a j o r a n d E m i n o r
G major

These scale patterns cover two octaves. Every F is sharpened in both scales.

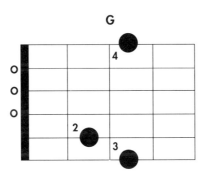

E m i n o r
(Relative minor of G major)

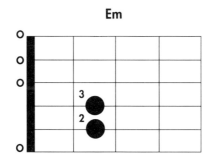

Now let's play a tune in the key of G using the scale fingering just learned. The verse is in G major but notice that the middle changes to the relative minor, (E minor) though the scale fingering is of course the same for both. Before you start playing this we'll have a look through the part together.

First there is a four bar intro and then you start playing the verse which is played twice (look out for the repeat signs at the end of bar 8).

Next comes the middle which is in E minor and has three bars which contain quarter note rests (rest for one beat).

The third verse is interesting as it has the instruction "8 va" which means it is to be played one octave higher than written! It is played in the 12th position (first finger on 12th fret). The correct fretting is shown as always on the Tablature and the fingering is indicated above the notation. I think you'll like playing up the finger board and it will sound nice on this tune.

Here's a little example of the G scale fingering on the 12th fret.

* Note the first finger plays both F♯ on the 11th fret and G on the 12th fret.

Now play around with the G scale in that 12th position and get comfortable with it.

After the third verse the repeat signs direct us back to the start of the middle from where we play right through to the end, giving you the chance once more of playing the 8 va verse. Look out for the last four bars which are back down in first position. OK, why not follow along with the cassette?

HOW STRANGE THE CHANGE

Hank Marvin

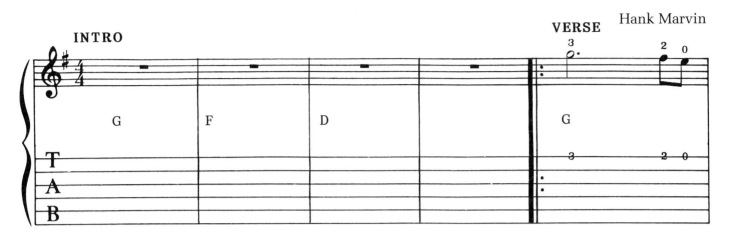

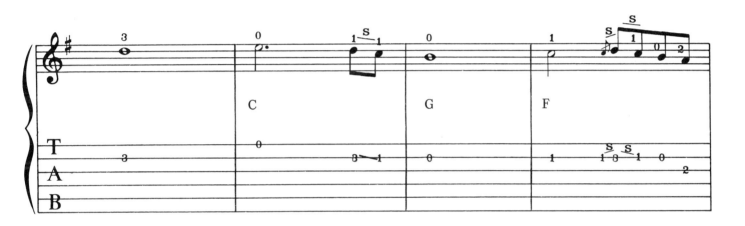

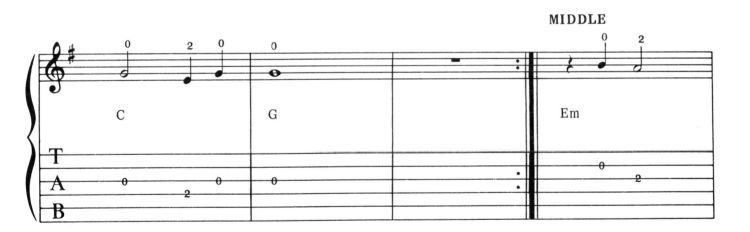

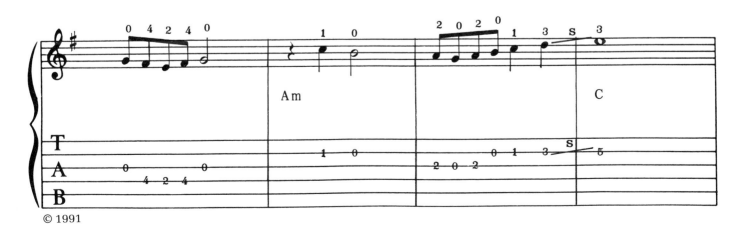

© 1991

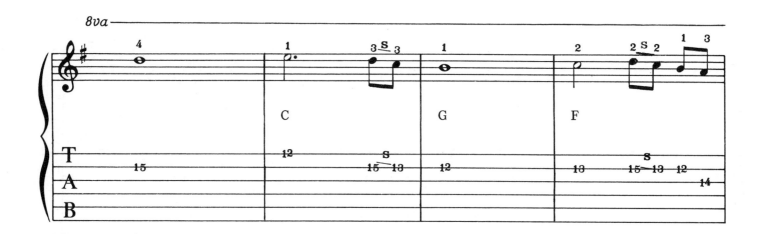

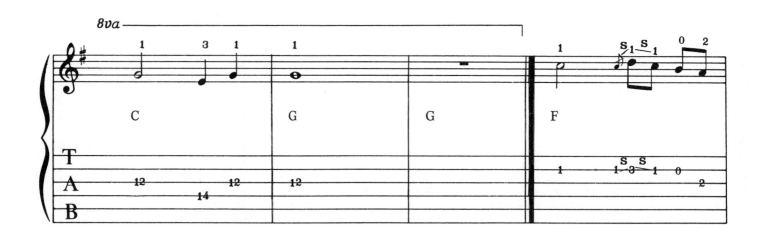

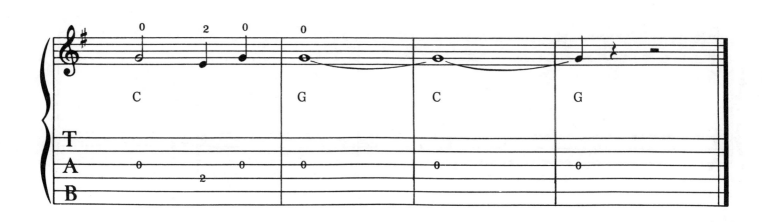

D MAJOR AND B MINOR

Now let's move on to the scales of **D major and it's relative minor, B minor,** which have the key signature of two sharps, indicating that in these scales both F and C are sharpened. There's also a little change in the fingering here so we'll examine that before you start to play.

If you compare the fingering indicated above the notes with the Tablature you'll notice that the fret numbers are no longer the same as the fingering. Well this is no cause for panic! It simply means that we have to move the left hand from the 1st position, which we have been using, to the 2nd position by moving it up one fret so that the first finger will be pressing the strings down on the second fret instead of the first as before.

D major

These scale patterns cover one octave, (D to D) and (B to B) respectively plus some notes of the next octave. Every F and C are sharpened.

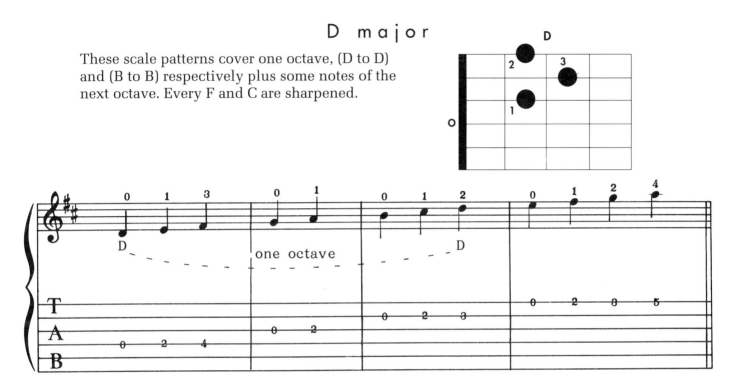

B major
(Relative minor of D major)

Barre chord version.
The first finger holds down the 1st and 5th strings like a bar pressing across the strings.

easier chord fingering

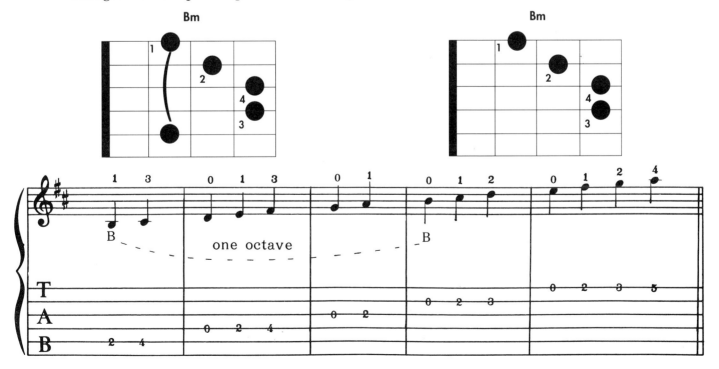

A MAJOR AND F♯ MINOR

The A major and F♯ minor scales have three sharps, F, D and G, and the fingering is again in the first position - except for the last three notes in the A scale where we move up one fret to the second position.

A major

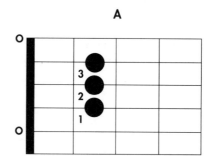

These scale patterns cover two octaves. Every F, C and G are sharpened in both scales.

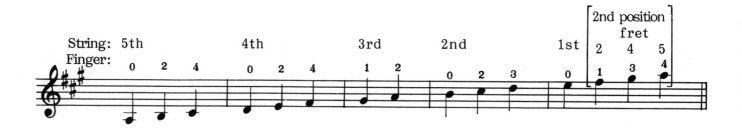

F♯ minor
(Relative minor of A major)

Barre chord version.
The 1st finger holds down all six strings on the 2nd fret. If this is too difficult at the moment (and I'll be surprised if it isn't!), try barring only the first three strings.

easier chord shape

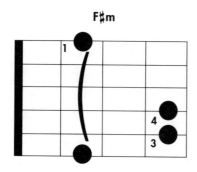

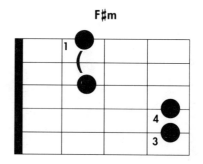

The scales of E major and C♯ minor have a key signature of four sharps F, C, G and D and the fingering is all in the first position, fret and finger numbers the same.

E major

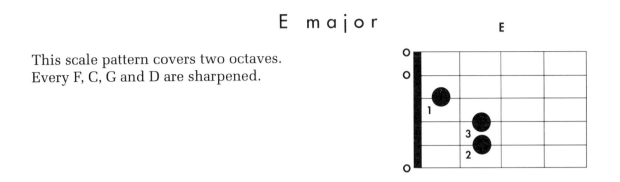

This scale pattern covers two octaves.
Every F, C, G and D are sharpened.

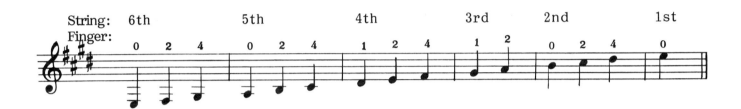

C♯ minor
(Relative minor of E major)

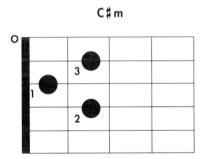

This scale pattern covers only one octave (C♯ to C♯) plus four notes of the next octave.
Every F, C, G and D are sharpened.

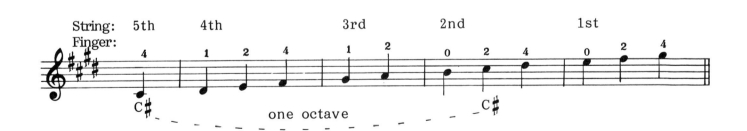

There are three more sharp keys which we won't concern ourselves with at the moment except for mentioning their names and key signatures.

B major (G♯m)
5 sharps

F♯ major (D♯m)
6 sharps

C♯ major (A♯m)
7 sharps

As well as sharp keys there are of course flat keys and they too have key signatures to indicate which notes in the scale are flattened or lowered. On the guitar a note is flattened by playing it one fret lower. There are also seven flat keys just as there are seven sharp keys.

F MAJOR AND D MINOR

These keys have a signature of one flat.

F major

This scale pattern covers two octaves.
Every B is flattened

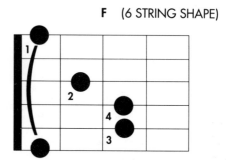

F   (6 STRING SHAPE)

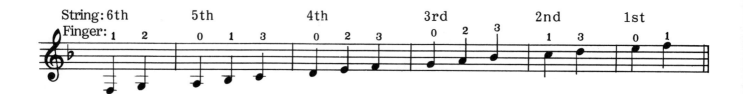

D minor
(Relative minor of F major)

This scale pattern covers one octave plus additional notes.
Every B is flattened.

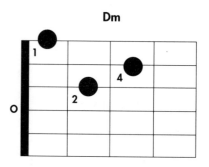

Dm

These keys have the signature of two flats.

B♭ MAJOR

This scale pattern covers one octave plus additional notes from the next octave. Every B and E are flattened.

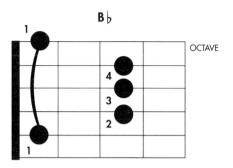

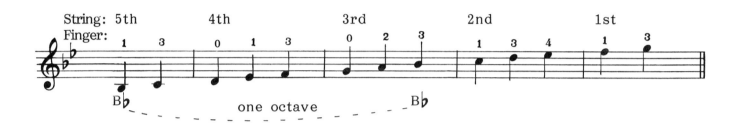

G MINOR
(Relative minor of B♭ major)

If on looking at this chord shape you get a feeling of deja vu, don't worry, they can't touch you for it and yes you have seen it before, but where? Well it is exactly the same shape as the F♯ minor you learned earlier, only this time it is played in the third position ie on the 3rd fret.

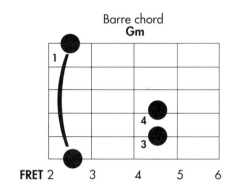

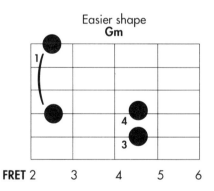

Two octaves are covered in this scale pattern.

There are five more flat keys which we'll leave alone except for naming them and noting their key signatures.

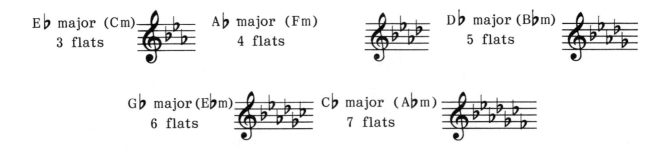

Eb major (Cm) — 3 flats   Ab major (Fm) — 4 flats   Db major (Bbm) — 5 flats

Gb major (Ebm) — 6 flats   Cb major (Abm) — 7 flats

You may well have found all these different key signatures and scales less than inspiring but knowing the relationship between the major keys and their relative minors is important and you can always refer back to that section if necessary. Shall we learn another tune?

This next tune is a 12 bar blues which is played in the same feel as the Shadows "The Rise and Fall of Flingel Bunt". It has a repetitive melody which is built on notes from "The Blues Scale", a scale that is used a lot in Rock, Blues and Jazz so it's really worth getting to know well.

Just before you start learning the tune let's have a look at the scale pattern we'll be using in the first verse. As you can see from the diagram and Tablature below there are no open strings used, which (apart from the G scale in the 12th position) is quite different to the scale patterns we've considered so far. This in fact is an advantage because it is a **moveable scale pattern** which I'll explain in a moment.

THE BLUES SCALE
(A moveable pattern)

The blues scale is made up of the following notes taken from the major scale. The root or tonic: Flat 3rd: 4th: Flat 5th: 5th and Flat 7th. Which in the key of C looks like this.

Here are two different patterns for a blues scale and it's on these that our next tune is played.

PATTERN ONE

Looks like this in musical notation.

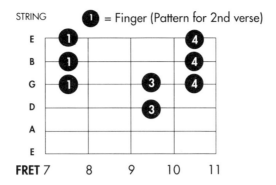

(C Blues scale)
Looks like this in musical notation

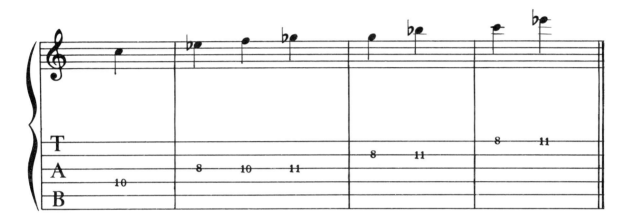

You may be wondering why I'm giving you these patterns in symbol form as well as in musical notation, well this is because on the guitar it is possible to transpose into any key without changing the fingering, but to do that we need to have available to use **moveable scale patterns,** and that's exactly what those blues scale fingerings are.

For example if you played either pattern one fret up it would become the B blues scale.

If you moved pattern One to the 7th fret, your first finger would be on an E on the 5th string and you'd be playing an E blues scale.

Let's try some practical examples

1) Play an E7 chord then with the sound of the chord in your mind play the pattern one blues scale on the seventh fret and hear the relationship.

2) Now try it with a B7 chord, the pattern one scale in the second position and the pattern two in the seventh position.

So you see **you can use these patterns anywhere on the fingerboard and play in any key.**

Later on we'll take a look at moveable forms of major, minor and flat 7 scales but right now **check out the blues scale with the cassette,** get the feel of the fingering, **remembering it is a moveable fingering pattern** and the we'll start learning our next tune, "The Secret Life of Squimby Nurox".

THE SECRET LIFE OF SQUIMBY NUROX

Hank Marvin

First we have a 12 bar intro then you join in playing the first verse, the fingering of
which is based on the pattern one blues scale in the 3rd position.

Repeat signs indicate that Bars one to four of the verse are played twice. (Although the
chord changes are different 2nd time, see the part). Look at bar two of the verse. It would
be nice to slide into that first note, making it a quick slide starting on the F two frets
below.

After the repeat go straight into the last four bars.

Now turn on the cassette and I'll help you learn this bar by bar.

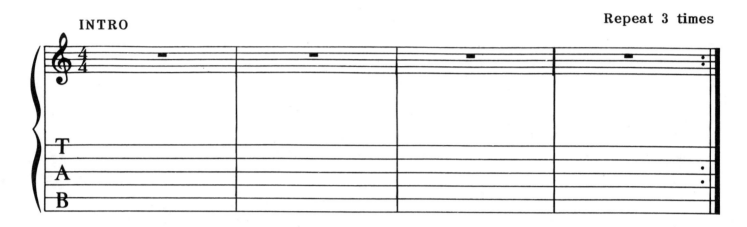

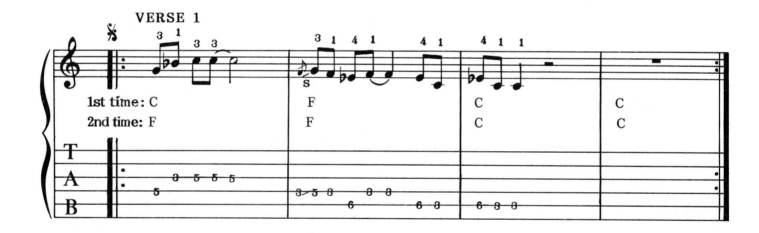

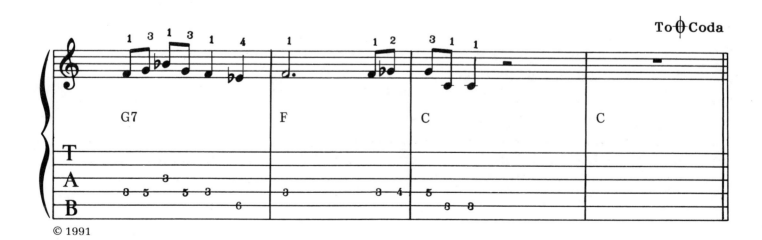

When you have learned verse one we'll take a look at the second verse, the fingering of
which is the pattern two blues scale in the 8th position.

SECOND VERSE

For the second verse you play exactly the same tune as the first only one octave higher. The fingering of course is different, taken this time from the pattern two blues scale.

As with verse one the first four bars are repeated and then on into the last four. Let's go through it together.

THE MIDDLE

The middle is played in the same position and uses the same fingering pattern as the second verse. Just look out for the quarter note (one beat) rests beginning bars one and five. OK we'll now learn the middle.

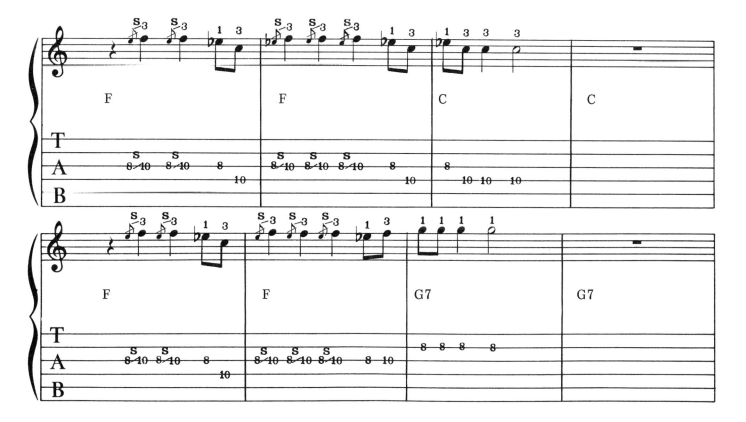

THE SOLO

After the middle we come back to another verse but rather than actually playing that it would be nice instead to solo over the chords, so we have here a little solo for you that I think you'll enjoy playing.

The first bar is the same fingering as the 2nd verse and middle but the next bar is interesting. Take a look and see how **in the 2nd bar we change the fingering to accommodate some slides.**

a) The third finger slides up on the 3rd string from it's previous position on the 10th fret to the 12th and while in that position the second finger can easily play the B♭ on the 2nd string 11th fret.

b) Then for the next four notes the third finger slides back to the 10th fret and stays in position until the last two notes in the bar where once again we slide up to the 12th fret as in a).

c) End the phrase with the first finger playing C on the 4th string 10th fret.

d) **The last two notes Bar six** and first note on bar seven are played the same as directed in procedures a) and c).

e) **Last two notes Bar seven** slide first finger on the 3rd string down from the 10th fret to the 8th.

We'll go through this slowly on the cassette.

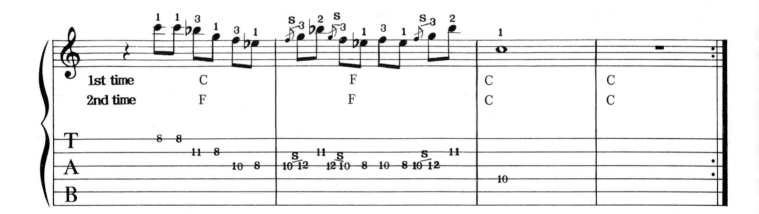

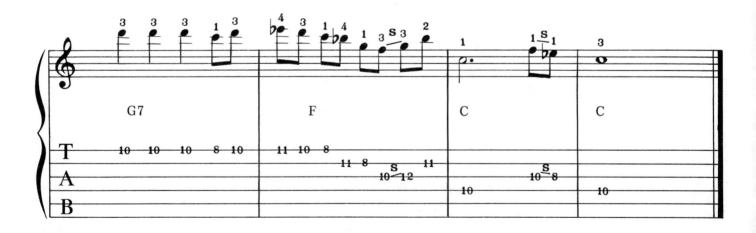

THE BRIDGE (DRUM BREAKS)

We now come to the bridge where the drummer takes the spotlight and the guitar plays a driving "Rock 'n' Blues riff in the Chuck Berry style (or the Status Quo style depending on how old you are). This calls for a bit of a stretch of the left hand fingers which are in the eighth position. Don't be too concerned if you can't make the stretch right away, it usually takes a little time, and practice to get it clean and solid.

Note that the lowest note in the riff stays on the same note through the whole bar, the top note only changing.

The fingering "shape" is as in the diagram, with the first and third fingers holding down their notes throughout the riff, only releasing during the drum fills and to change chords, for example into bars five and seven.

The fourth finger alternatively presses and releases the string to allow the top note to change every beat. Let's go for it.

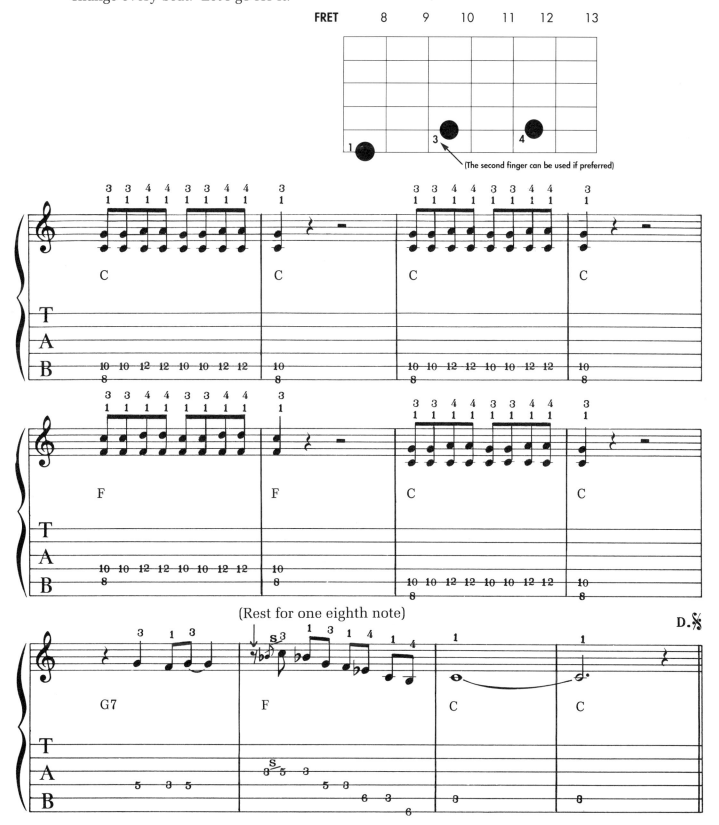

THE LAST VERSE AND ENDING

You'll be glad to know that we've virtually got the whole piece together now, because all that's left is the last verse, which is just the first verse repeated, and the ending.

The ending is similar to the intro but without the four bars of drums that we have at the beginning. Also you join in and play the concluding phrase which is identical to the one you play at the end of the Bridge. Check these out and try to put the whole thing together.

If, by the way, you're trying to memorise what you're learning rather than tying yourself to the music, that's good, because eventually you'll want to be able to play lots of tunes without having to depend on having the sheet music, being able to play what you want, when you want.

Having said all that, it's still useful to know a bit about reading music, so let's check out some commonly used symbols that I haven't referred to yet although you probably noticed them. For example at the end of the Bridge:

D.S.   This **means** that when you reach that place in the music you **go back to the sign,** which looks like this, 𝄋 and play from that point once more.

So you go back and play through the first verse from the sign and just when you think it's safe to carry one, up pops a hot cross bun with a sign saying "TO CODA".⊕

TO CODA   Look down at the ending and you'll see another of these hot cross buns which this time claims to be the CODA,⊕. Go straight to it and play on from there to the end. That then is the procedure for following these symbols.

THE ENDING (CODA)

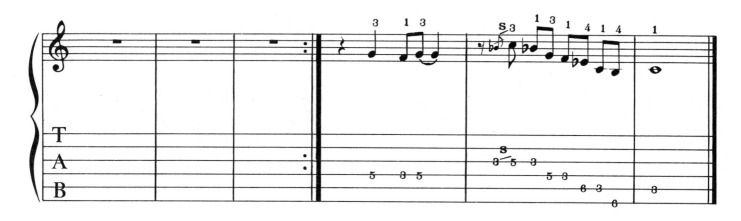

MOVEABLE SCALE PATTERNS

When I started to learn the guitar I wanted to be able to play up the fingerboard away from the first position, but all the scales I'd come across in the guitar books were played down there using open strings! Well I figured out that it was possible to work out the scale patterns with no open strings, which meant that I could use them anywhere on the fingerboard, in other words **moveable scale patterns**. Of course if I had gone to a guitar teacher (or had a book like this) I would have been shown all this and saved a lot of time and effort. So I'd like to show you some of these scale patterns and encourage you to really learn and practise them because whatever kind of music you eventually get into, rock, country or jazz etc you'll be playing off scales of one kind or another.

MAJOR SCALE PATTERNS (ONE OCTAVE)

Note that patterns one to three cover the same register in different positions.

These are all C major scale patterns

Pattern One (2nd pos)

* Alternative fingering (Pattern Two)
Use **either** 4th finger on the 9th fret.
or 1st finger on 4th fret.

Pattern Two (5th pos)

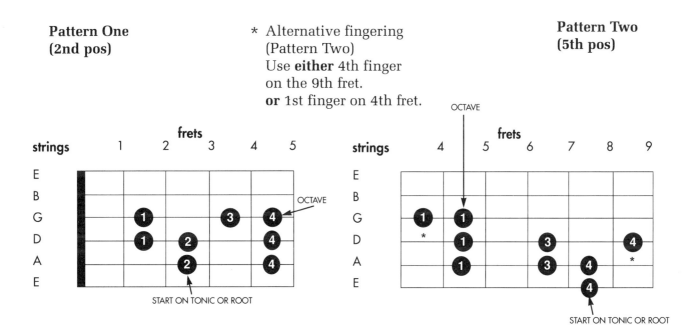

Pattern Three (7th pos)

Practise all patterns slowly and accurately in every position up to the 12th fret using alternate picking.

Pattern Four (12th pos)

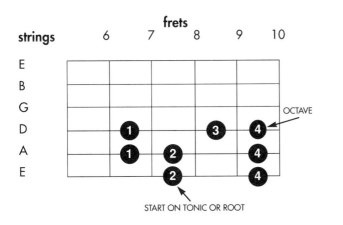

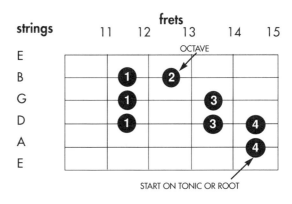

EXTENDED MOVEABLE SCALE PATTERNS

These basic scale patterns can all be extended to more than one octave in some cases to more than two octaves, which is very useful for positional playing. The scales are extended by adding notes above the first octave and sometimes adding notes below the root or tonic.

Remember these patterns are just an extension of the basic one octave patterns you've already learned so you're just adding to what you already know. Practise them until you are familiar with the fingering and try also to hear the relationship between the different notes in the scale.

MAJOR SCALE PATTERNS

These are all C major scale patterns

**Pattern One
(2nd Pos)**

Start all patterns on the tonic
play to the top note,
then back down to
notes below before
coming back to the tonic.

**Pattern Two
(5th Pos)**

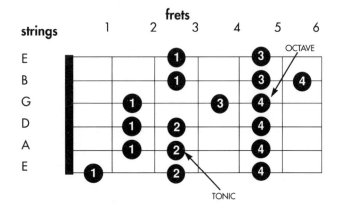

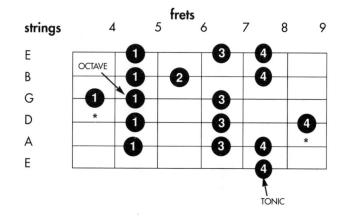

In pattern one we don't quite cover two octaves of the scale but we do go down a 5th below the root or tonic (key note), down to a low F. We also go up a 6th above the first octave to an A.

Pattern two covers the whole two octaves.

Pattern three covers two octaves with a half step below the root (key note) and a whole step above the high octave that we call the 9th.

Pattern four covers only one octave plus a sixth below and a fifth above.

**Pattern Three
(7th Pos)**

**Pattern Four
(12th Pos)**

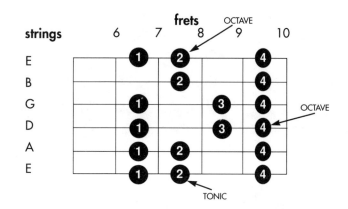

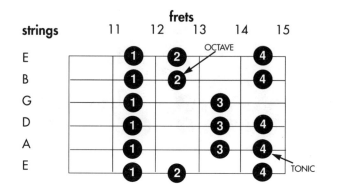

BROKEN HILL

PLAY A TUNE USING SCALE PATTERN FINGERING

I'm sure that now you'd like to learn another tune and put into practice some of those scale pattern fingerings we've discussed, so let's do that right away with a piece of music written in $^3/_4$ TIME.

Remember, $^3/_4$ time has three quarter notes (crotchets) to the bar, so we **count three beats to the bar like this:**

Count: 1   2   3   1   2   3   1 & 2   3   1   2   3   1   2   3

Looking at the music you'll see that it's written in the key of G (one sharp). There is a **four bar intro** where you play nothing (of course if you want to make up a little intro figure, great, go ahead).

VERSES ONE AND TWO

Play these verses on the lower three strings (D,A and E) **using pattern three G major scale fingering** which is in the 2nd position (1st finger, 2nd fret). Bars 6, 10 and 12 have finger slides where the fingering is changed to make it smoother. (The last note fingering in Bar 10 is also altered in preparation for the slide in the following bar).

The slides in bars 6 and 10 are upward and you start from the same fret with the same finger used for the previous melody note in each case.

Bar 12 is different, the slide is downward from D to B on the 5th string and it brings the first finger back into position.

Don't miss the repeat sign at the end of the verse and as you play through the **second time, take the second time bars not the first.**

THE MIDDLE

The middle is played on the top three strings (E, B and G) alternating between the 5th and 7th positions **using the major scale pattern four fingering.** Bars one and two are played in the 5th position and bars three and four in the 7th, the slide in the second bar (3rd string C, up to D) takes the first finger up to the 7th fret. The next four bars (five to eight) repeat this.

The section from bar nine to the end, although changing position as before, is a little different melodically. The notes in bar eleven are held over to form a three part chord in bar twelve (which is in the 7th Pos) and we stay in that position to the end of the middle.

THE LAST VERSE AND ENDING

Apart from the first three notes we move **back to pattern three fingering** in the second position as we were in the first two verses. Played on the top four strings (E, B, G and D) this is melodically the same as the second verse until bar sixteen where we have a little pick up leading into the coda. The coda repeats the last phrase in the verse over the F and D chords then concludes with an arpeggio and chord of G major. By the way, I've put the slides in different places in this verse to show you other possibilities. Go through this with the cassette.

BROKEN HILL

Verse 1 & 2   Hank Marvin

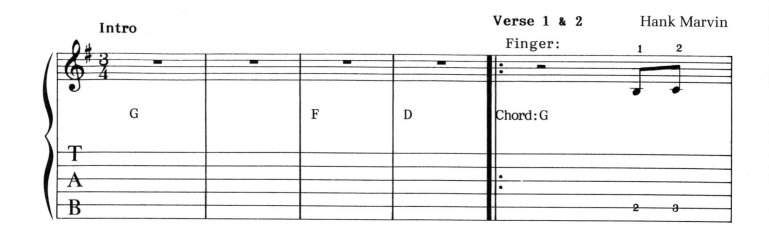

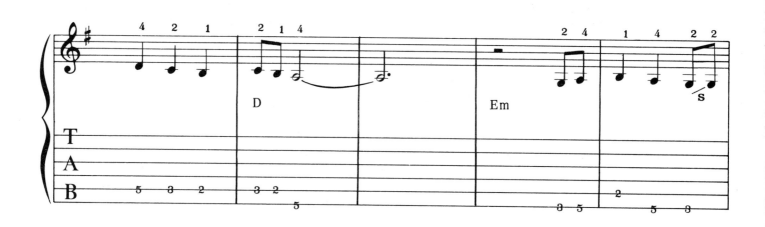

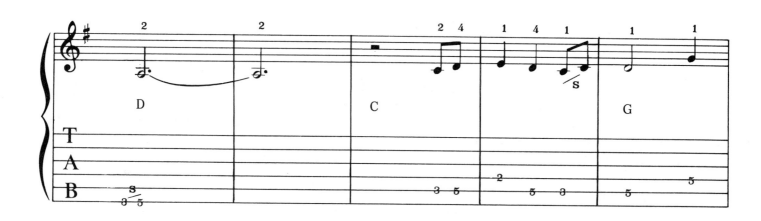

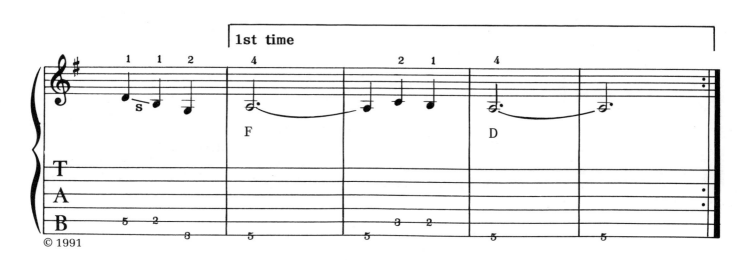

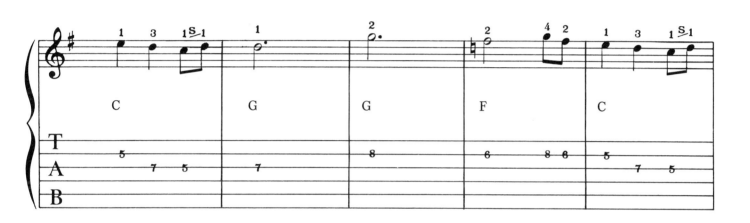

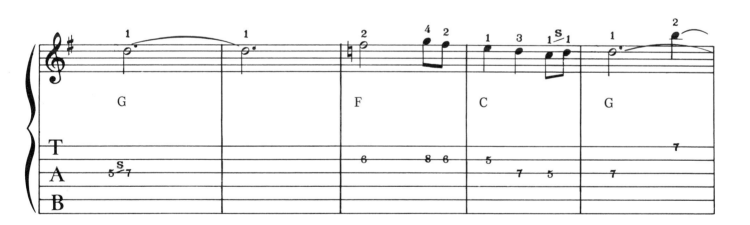

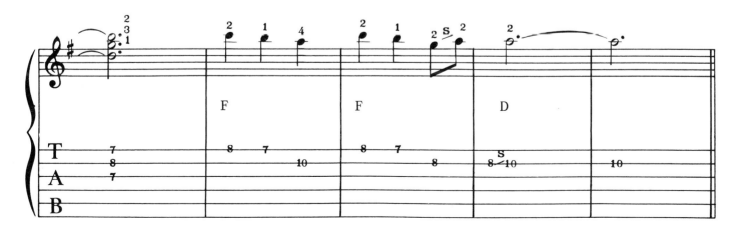

LAST VERSE 1

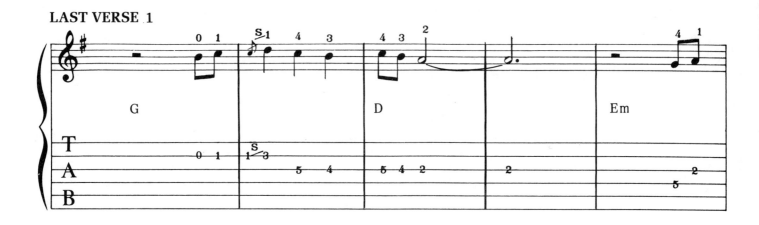

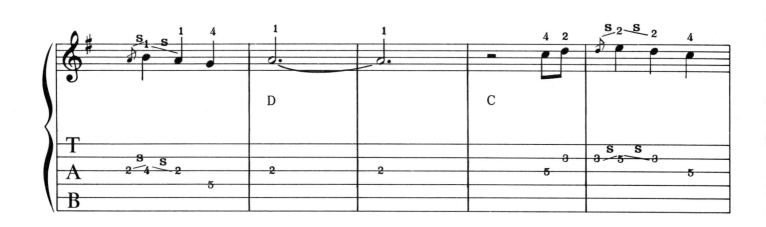

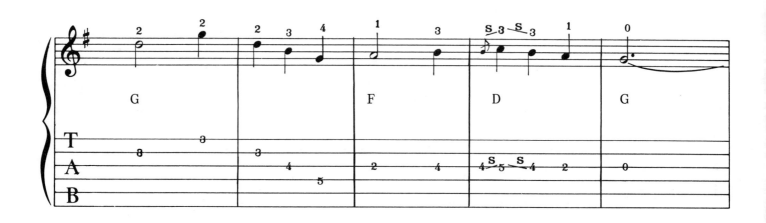

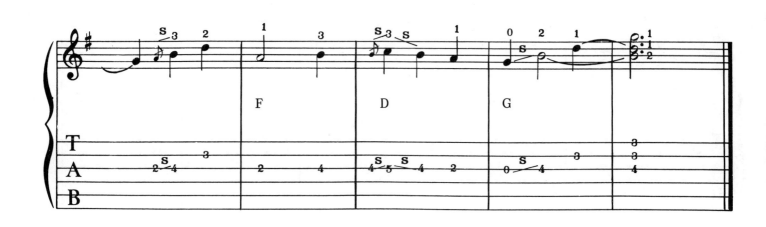

MOVEABLE MINOR SCALE PATTERNS
(ONE OCTAVE)

Let's take a look at four natural minor scale patterns using the relative minor of C major which is A minor. Note that patterns one and two although in different positions are in the same octave. The fingering for these patterns is derived from the major scales we've already discussed so it should feel familiar to you. Keep in mind though that the relative minor starts on the sixth tone of the major scale so the tonic will fall under a different finger.

Pattern One (2nd Pos)　　　　　　　　　　　　　　**Pattern Two ((5th Pos)**

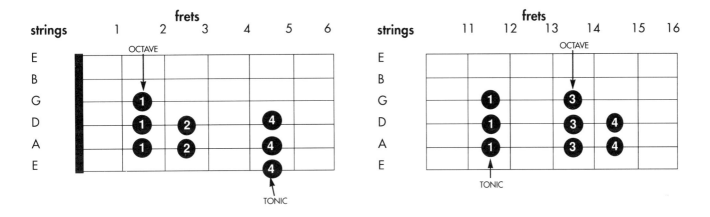

Patterns three and four are in this key an octave higher.

Pattern Three　　　　　　　　　　　　　　　　　　**Pattern Four**
(7th Position)　　　　　　　　　　　　　　　　　　**(12th Position)**

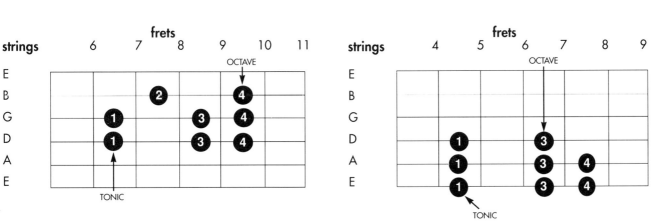

Here are four extended scale patterns for the key of A minor, (the relative minor of C major)

Once again start the scale on the tonic and play up to the highest note, then play back down the scale to the notes below the tonic, finishing off by playing from the low notes back up to the tonic.

Now let's see how patterns one and two look as Two Octave scales. I'll be right along with you on the cassette.

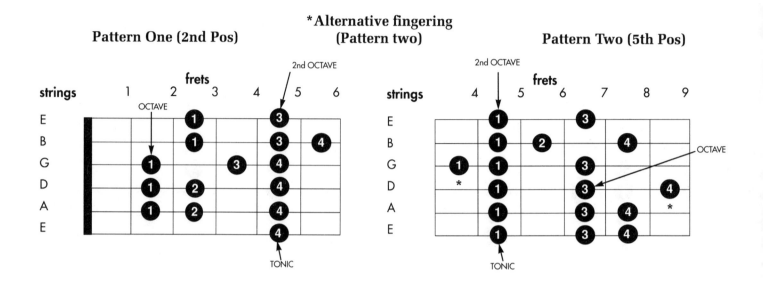

Pattern three doesn't cover two whole octaves of the scale, it only goes up to a fourth above the first octave and down a whole step below the tonic or root (key note).

Pattern four doesn't quite cover two octaves of the scale but goes up to the seventh above the first octave which is one note below the second octave and down a whole step below the tonic.

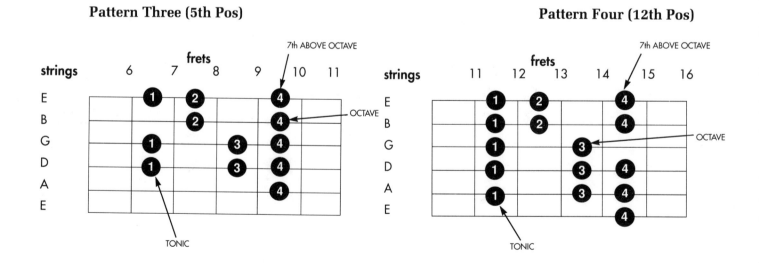

These examples of scale patterns in different positions may help you appreciate how easy it is to play in any key by using moveable patterns.

The **first example** is of the **pattern three major scale** where for simplicity I've shown the **first octave fingering only**. The scale pattern is shown in three positions, 1st position (F♯ scale); 7th position (C scale) and 14th position (G scale). With this pattern the scale starts on the second finger, 6th string.

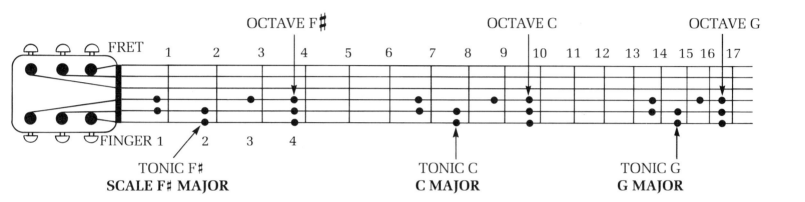

This next example is of the **pattern four minor scale**, again for simplicity showing **only the first octave fingering** in three different positions.

We have it shown in the 2nd position (B minor); 7th position (E minor) and 12th position (A minor), with this pattern the scale starts with the first finger 5th string.

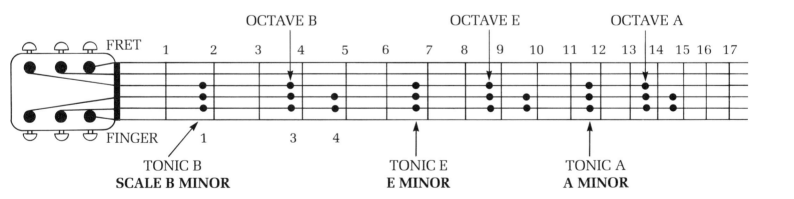

Using these scale patterns in conjunction with your fingerboard note chart you can do a lot of enjoyable exploring and discovering.

Practise all the major and minor scale patterns each day using the down/up picking technique and be amazed at your progress both in technique and knowledge of the fingerboard.

BINGLE SOUNDS

Hank Marvin

This tune is in he key of E minor (one sharp) and is played using the pattern four minor scale fingering in the seventh position. There is a four bar intro played over an E min. chord and then the lead guitar (you!) comes in playing the melody.

THE VERSE

The verse is eight bars in length and is played on the top four string of the guitar. The melodic phrase played in the first two bars is also played in bars three and four, so you just learn the first two bar phrase and play it twice. At the end of the verse play the "first time bars" and obeying the repeat signs play through the verse again, this time playing the "second time bars". Look out for the quarter note (one beat) rests in bars two, four and six.

THE MIDDLE

In the second time bars there is an ascending run on the first three strings leading in to the middle where you will notice there are several dotted notes. Remember this increases the value of the note by half. In bar one for example, the first note, a dotted half note, is held for three beats There are also two lots of tied notes, remember to play tied notes as one long note. The last bar of the middle has a phrase to lead us into the third verse.

THE THIRD VERSE

Although the melody is the same as the other verses we play it an octave lower still using the pattern four minor scale fingering. At the end of the last bar which contains the ascending run in to the middle look out for the **D.S.** indicating you go back to and play from the **Sign 𝄋** which is the second middle.
 Notice that at the end of bar nine we go **TO CODA.**

THE CODA

Go straight to the CODA where you play the lead in to the verse, the last verse in the high octave and then the ending.
 The only difference between the last four bars of the verse and the ending is the phrase played over the E min chord on the very last two bars.
 Now turn on the cassette and we'll go through this together.

BINGLE SOUNDS

Hank Marvin

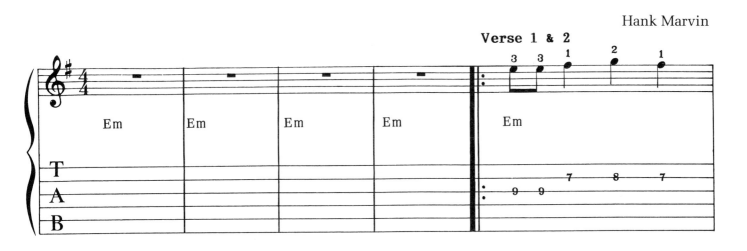

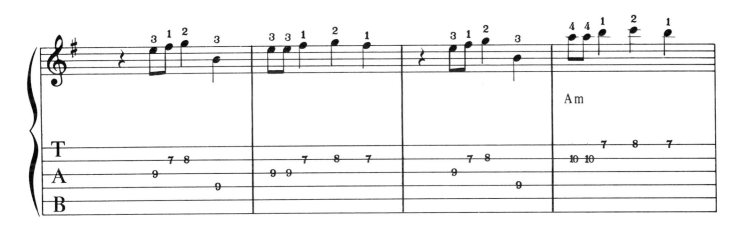

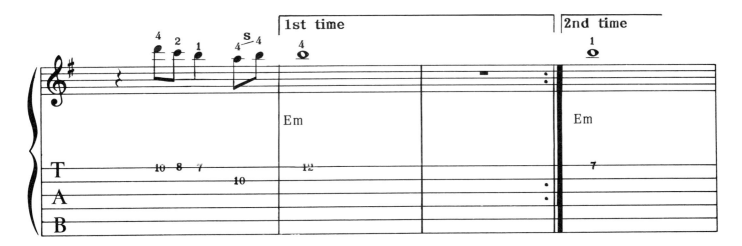

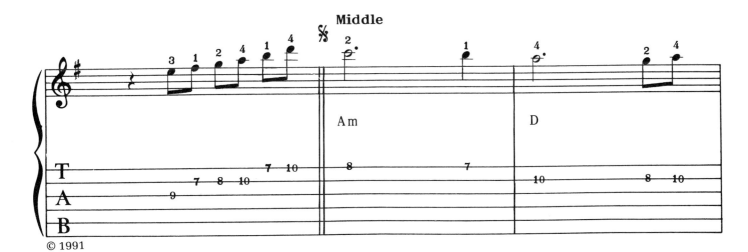

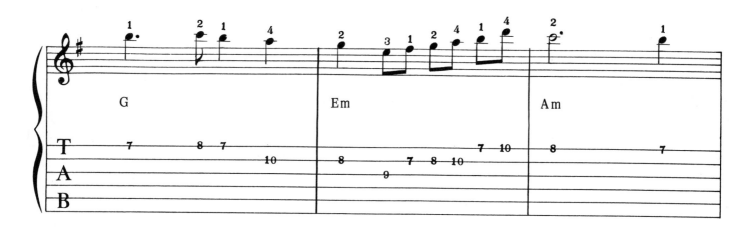

Verse 3

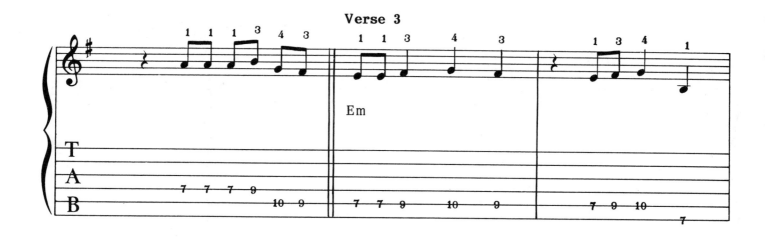

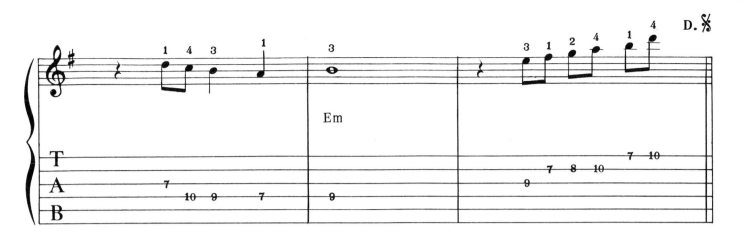

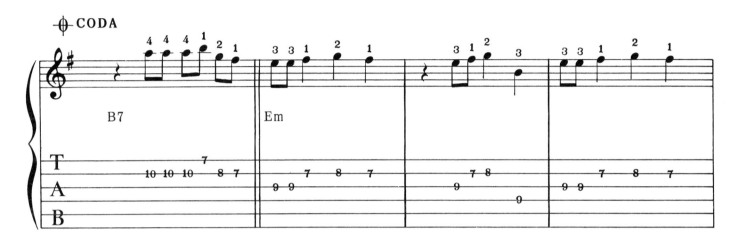

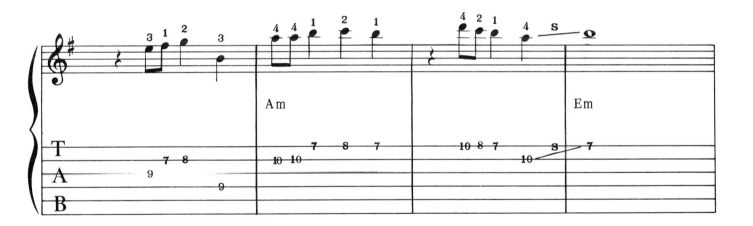

STRING BENDING

String bending is used in most modern styles of guitar playing and will add a new dimension and expression to your playing. It's basically a matter of pushing or pulling a string across the fingerboard so that the pitch is raised to a higher note. In order to control the string bend and give more strength to it, we need to employ a slightly different left hand technique to the one we've been using, one which brings the thumb round the neck of the guitar. This presents no problem because it's easy to switch from one technique to the other, even in the same piece of music.

(1) Bring the thumb right round the neck of the guitar so that it's sticking out (like a sore thumb) and move your hand to the 12th position. Play G on the 3rd string with the 1st finger, then A with your 3rd and then with your 1st and 2nd fingers also on the same string to give strength, push the A up a whole step (tone) tc B and then let it slowly drop back and finish on the G (Ex.1)

(X = Add finger to assist the bend)

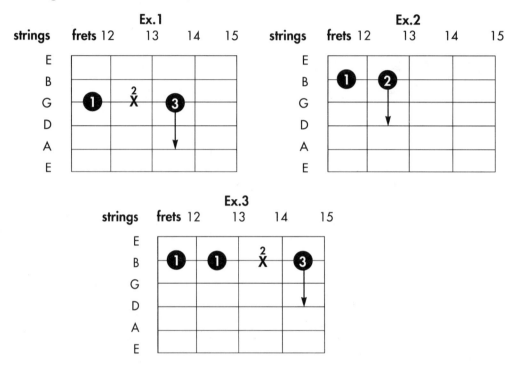

(2) Still in the 12th position play the B on the 2nd string with your 1st finger then the C on the same string with the 2nd. Now with the 1st finger still on the string to give added strength to the 2nd, push the string up to raise it a whole step to D. Lower it slowly back to C and finish on the B 1st finger. (Ex.2).

(3) Again on the 2nd string, 12th fret play the B with the 1st finger, then move it up a position and play the C also with the 1st and then the D with the 3rd finger. Now with the 1st and 2nd fingers also helping, push the string up a whole step to E, lower it slowly back to D and play C, 1st finger then B, 1st finger to finish (Ex.3).

(4) Play E on the 1st string with the 1st finger then F♯ with the 3rd, now push up the F♯ a half step (semi-tone) to G with the 1st and 2nd fingers helping the 3rd. Lower it slowly back to F♯ and finish on E. (Ex.4).

Listen to the demonstration on the cassette.

Hammering on and **Pulling off** are techniques that you should learn, so here are a couple of exercises that will help you. Hammering on is simply where you pick one note and by "hammering" another left hand finger down on to the string you play another note without using the pick. It's highly usable, have a listen to the cassette and I'll demonstrate.

EXERCISE (1)
Start in the 3rd position and play CHART (1), picking the first note and hammering the second with the 2nd finger. Work across all the strings as shown and go up and down the fingerboard as we did with the other exercises.

EXERCISE (1a)
This time hammer with the 3rd finger onto the 5th fret, CHART (1a) and repeat the above procedure.

EXERCISE (1b)
Same again except the 4th finger is now used to hammer on as in CHART (1b).
The "Daily Warm Up Exercises" (1) and (2) can also be used, pick only the first note on each string (in each position of course) and hammer the rest.

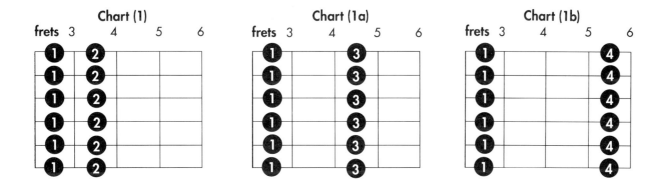

Pulling off is the opposite of Hammering on. With this technique you pick or hammer the note first and then pull your finger off the string in such a way that it almost picks the next note which a lower placed finger is fretting. I'll also demonstrate this on the cassette.

EXERCISE (2)
This incorporates both techniques because we pull off the note and then hammer back onto it. Start in the 12th position on the first string and work down on the three high strings missing out the lower strings until your fingers get stronger. Pick the high G and then pull the 4th finger off the string to make the high E ring out, hammer it on again and the G should ring. Repeat this with the other fingering shown on CHART (2) in all positions.

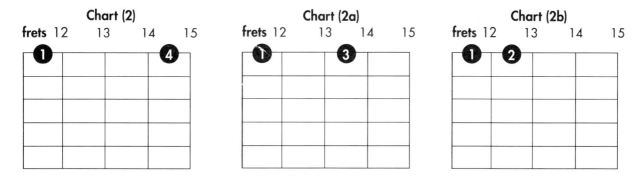

Play all the above on the 1st string before moving to the 2nd and 3rd.

BLUES SCALE EXTENDED PATTERNS

The two blues scale patterns you already know are the most commonly used ones and can be extended to play two octaves across all six strings, so here are the patterns for those plus a variation pattern for each, which I think you'll find very useful. We'll again show them as the C blues scale.

Pattern one (Pos 3)

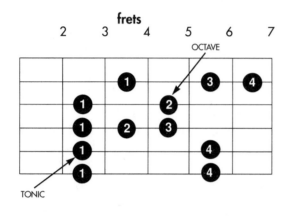

Pattern two (Pos 8)

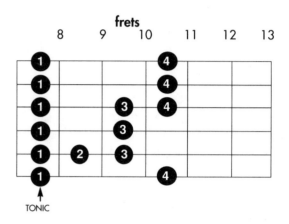

Pattern one extension variation (Pos 3 and 5)
1st finger moves between Positions 3 and 5 on 3rd string

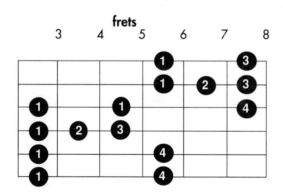

Pattern two extension variation (Pos 8 and 10)
1st finger moves between Positions 8 and 10 on 4th string

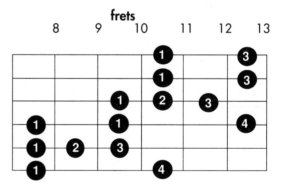

Practise pattern one first, then the extension and finally both together, going smoothly from one to the other. When that feels good, do the same with pattern two and its extension.

As with the previous patterns, practise these in all positions.

The thought of practising exercises can make some people feel very unwell, but if you really want to improve and get your playing up to a good standard, you've got to have a positive attitude. Look ahead and be determined to develop your talent while enjoying the greater ability that exercises and practising will give you.

Here are just a few exercises to improve both left and right hand technique:

EXERCISE (1)

Starting with a low F♯ on the 6th string, play four ascending notes per string as in CHART (1), on hitting the last and highest note, (A) on the 1st string, move up one fret and starting from there play the whole thing in reverse, ie descending fingering 4, 3, 2, 1.

On reaching the low G move up one fret and starting on G♯ do exactly the same again. Repeat this all the way up to the 12th position and back down to the 2nd. Play this all the way up to the 12th position and back down to the 2nd. Play this and all exercises slowly and accurately, speed will come naturally.

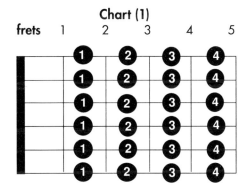

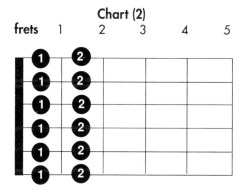

EXERCISE (1a)

This is simply a variation on Ex.(1). Start as before and ascend on alternate strings coming back one every time like this. Play the strings in this order.

6th, 4th, 5th, 3rd, 4th, 2nd, 3rd, 1st. Move up one fret then reverse it 1st, 3rd, 2nd, 4th, 3rd, 5th, 4th, 6th. Move up the fingerboard to the 12th fret as in Ex. (1). Play back down the same way.

EXERCISE (2)

Starting on the low F work your way across the fingerboard by playing a pattern of 1st and 2nd finger on frets 1 and 2 across all six strings and back again, then do the same with the 2nd and 3rd finger on frets 2 and 3 then this time with the 3rd and 4th fingers on frets 3 and 4 (and this will be difficult) but stick with it and you'll see the results. After doing that move up one position and with starting note F♯ repeat the procedure. Practise up to 12th position and back as in the previous exercises. CHART (2).

If you check out the cassette we'll run through all the exercises together.

RIGHT HAND EXERCISES

Good picking technique is an important factor not only in strawberry farming but in plectrum guitar playing, so it's worthwhile practising exercises to develop it. Here are a few to keep you busy.

EXERCISES (1-4)

This exercise uses the various scale patterns so you can practise those at the same time as you practise right hand technique. Using G major scale Pat.3 as an example, (that is in 2nd position, second finger plays G on 6th string). Play from the lowest tonic to the highest note and then descend back to the tonic using the following note values. Do this first in quarter notes (ex.1), then in eighth notes (Ex.2), eighth note triplets (Ex.3) and then sixteenth notes (Ex.4).

PLAY SLOWLY AND EVENLY

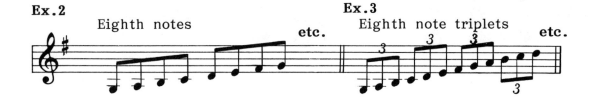

EXERCISE (5-7)

Using the scale patterns exactly as in Exercise (1) we now change the picking so that we alternate the note values within the scale. First we play the scale alternating between quarter and eighth notes (Ex.5), then quarter notes and eighth note triplets (Ex.6), and finally quarter and sixteenth notes (Ex.7).

PLAY FULL SCALE

Listen to the demonstration of these exercises on the cassette.

EXERCISE (8-11)

Quite often when playing guitar you find that you want to pick strings that are not adjacent, for example, 1st and 3rd, 2nd and 4th. So here's an exercise to help with that. I've shown it picked on an open E chord but you can use the same principle with any chord shape.

Pick the strings in the following order 6th - 4th; 5th - 3rd; 4th - 2nd; 3rd - 1st; 3rd - 2nd; 4th - 3rd; - 5th - 4th; 6th - 4th.

Play the exercise slowly and accurately, first of all in quarter notes, (Ex.8) has this written out in full. Then in eighth notes as in the abbreviated example in (Ex.9). In triplets as in (Ex.10) and finally in sixteenth notes as in (Ex.11).

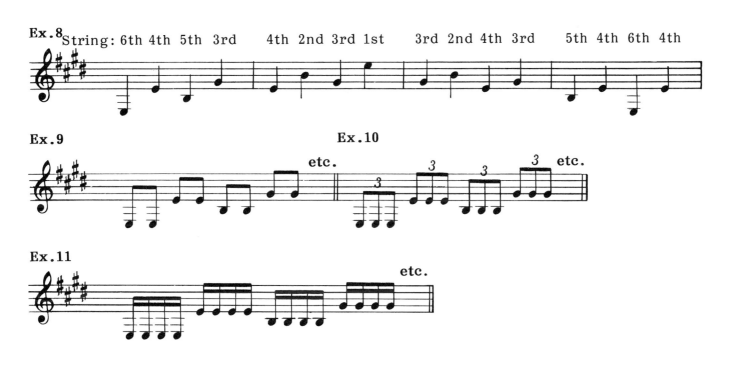

EXERCISE (12 & 12a)

This is to help develop a technique where instead of picking with down/up strokes, the pick is pulled in one direction, up or down, across several strings. It's good for fast little arpeggio runs. Keep the pick as near perpendicular to the strings as you can and pull it across in one smooth unbroken motion.

Start in the 12th position and work down the fingerboard with each example beginning with (Ex.12). I'll demonstrate these on the cassette.

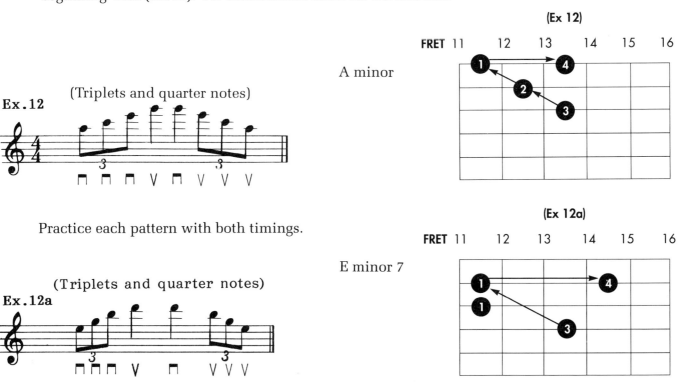

Practice each pattern with both timings.

MORE RIGHT HAND EXERCISES

Here are two exercises that will help your picking accuracy and are fun to play. The first is in the key of C and is played in the first position using some open strings. It has a kind of country music feel to it. The picking will be difficult at first so practise slowly aiming for clean accurate picking.

EXERCISE (13)

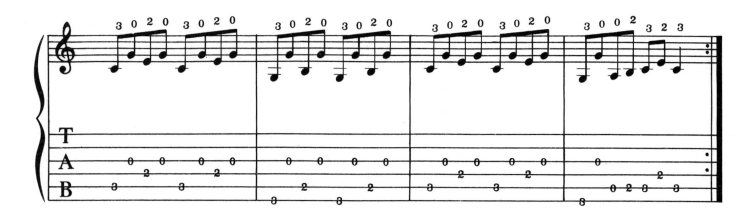

EXERCISE (14) is in the key of D and is best played with the first and third fingers maintaining their positions on the 3rd and 2nd strings respectively (see Tablature) and the second finger doing its thing on the 5th string. Talking of that, note that the fretted note on the 5th string is a C natural and not as might be expected in this key a C sharp. This gives it a more "blue" sound. Again practise slowly, and listen to the cassette.

Just as we have movable scale patterns that enable us to play in any key without changing fingering, so we have movable chord shapes that give us the same facility. A movable chord shape has no open strings and can be played in different positions on the fingerboard and as it is moved so it's name changes. As an example of this let's use two shapes you've already learned, the ones for F major and B minor.

If the F shape is played in the third position it becomes the chord of G major, taking its name from the note on the first string. In the fifth position it is A major. Take it up to the eighth position and you've got C major. Try this out and then compare the sound of these chord shapes with the open string versions your learned earlier.

G MAJOR

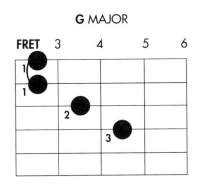

A MAJOR

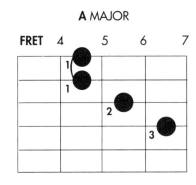

C MAJOR

Now, using the shape you learned for B minor, which was in the second position, move it up two frets to the fourth position and you have C♯minor, taking it's name from the note on the 5th string. Move it to the seventh position and it becomes E minor, in the tenth position you have G minor. As before compare these with the open string shapes learned earlier.

C♯ MINOR

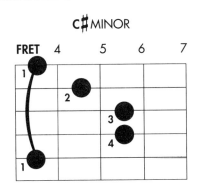

E MINOR

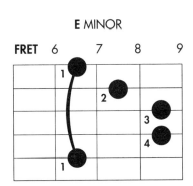

G MINOR

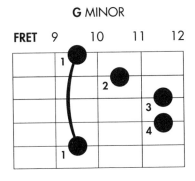

Following is a small selection of commonly used chord shapes that you can add to your repertoire over a period of time.

MAJOR CHORDS

Shape one	**Shape two**	**Shape three**
The name of this chord is the same as the note played on the 1st or 6th string.	The name of this chord is the same as the note played on the 5th string.	The name of this chord is the same as the note played on the 5th string.

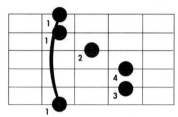 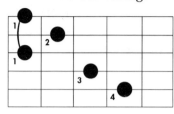 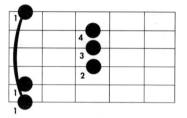

Four string version	Four string version	Four string version

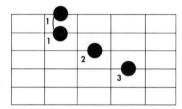 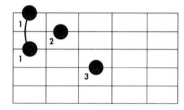 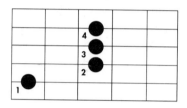

MAJOR SEVENTH CHORDS

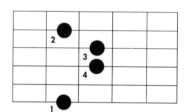 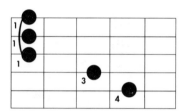 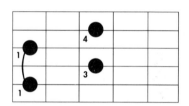

SEVENTH CHORDS

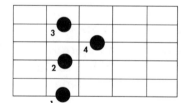 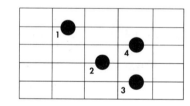 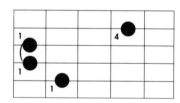

Six string version

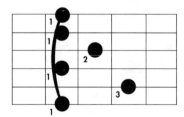

MAJOR SIXTH CHORDS

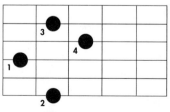 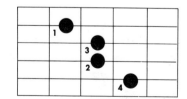 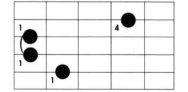

Alternative   Alternative

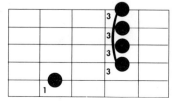

MINOR CHORDS

Shape one
The name of this chord is the same as the note played on the 1st or 6th string.

Shape two
The name of this chord is the same as the note played on the 4th string.

Shape three
The name of this chord is the same as the note played on the 5th string.

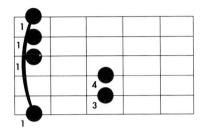

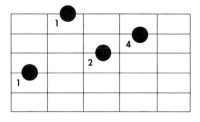

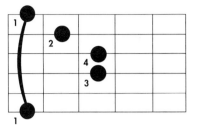

Four string version

Four string version

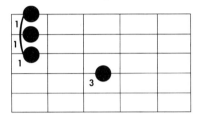

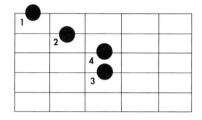

MINOR MAJOR SEVENTH CHORDS

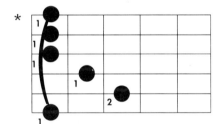

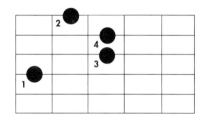

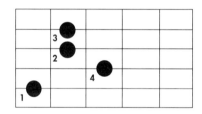

MINOR SEVENTH CHORDS

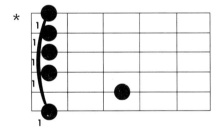

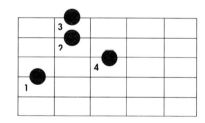

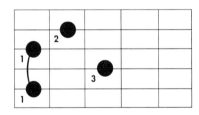

MINOR SIXTH CHORDS

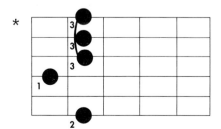

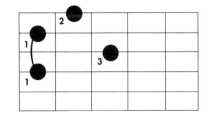

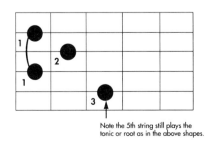

Note the 5th string still plays the tonic or root as in the above shapes.

* Play only first four strings for four string version

NINTH CHORDS

Shape one
The name of this chord is
the same as the note played
on the 6th string.

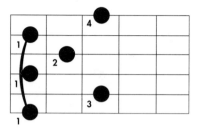

Shape two
The name of this chord is
the same as the note played
on the 4th string.

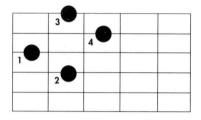

Shape three
The name of this chord is
the same as the note played
on the 5th string.

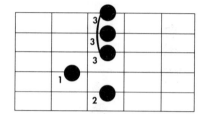

THIRTEENTH CHORDS

The name of this chord is
the same as the note played
on the 6th string.

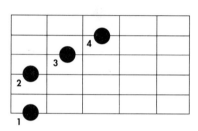

The name of this chord is
the same as the note played
on the 1st string.

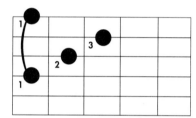

Shape three
The name of this chord is
the same as the note played
on the 5th string.

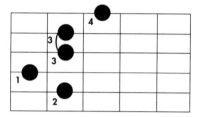

MINOR NINTH CHORDS

Shape one
The name of this chord is
the same as the note played
on the 6th string.

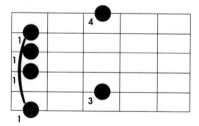

Shape two
The name of this chord is
the same as the note played
on the 6th string.

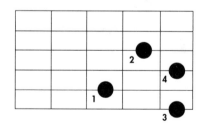

Shape three
The name of this chord is
the same as the note played
on the 5th string.

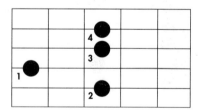

AUGMENTED CHORD

The names of these chords are the same as
the notes played on the following strings.

1st str.

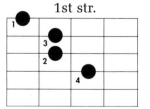

2nd str.

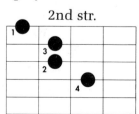

6th str.

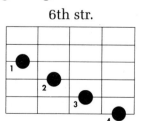

DIMINISHED CHORDS

The names of these chords can be taken
from a note on any string.

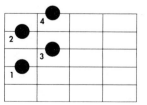

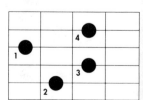

Although two of the augmented shapes are identical their tonic notes are found on
different strings and they are based on different major shapes, (shapes One and Two).

THE FINGERBOARD

You've probably realised by now that at times we've been playing the same notes on different strings and in other positions. Well this is one of the unusual things about the guitar, you see it's possible to play the same note in the same register in more than one place, sometimes in as many as five!

With this possibility in mind here's a very useful chart to show you the different places on the fingerboard where the same note can be played. So that we don't get too complicated the chart will show only the seven basic notes; A-B-C-D-E-F-G. Any note that can be played in only one position will not be shown.

1.

1) 5th string-open
2) 6th string-5th fret

1) 3rd string -2nd fret
2) 4th string -7th fret
3) 5th string - 12th fret
4) 6th string - 17th fret

1) 1st string - 5th fret
2) 2nd string - 10th fret
3) 3rd string - 14th fret
4) 4th string - 19th fret.

2.

1) 5th string - 2nd fret
2) 6th string - 7th fret

1) 2nd string - open
2) 3rd string - 4th fret
3) 4th string - 9th fret
4) 5th string - 14th fret
5) 6th string - 19th fret

1) 1st string - 7th fret
2) 2nd string - 12th fret
3) 3rd string - 16th fret
4) 4th string - 21st fret (your fingerboard may not go this high)

3.

1) 5th string - 3rd fret
2) 6th string - 8th fret

1) 2nd string - 1st fret
2) 3rd string - 5th fret
3) 4th string 10th fret
4) 5th string - 15th fret
5) 6th string - 20th fret

1) 1st string - 8th fret
2) 2nd string - 13th fret
3) 3rd string - 17th fret

4.
1) 4th string - open
2) 5th string - 5th fret
3) 6th string - 10th fret

1) 2nd string - 3rd fret
2) 3rd string - 7th fret
3) 4th string - 12th fret
4) 5th string - 17th fret

1) 1st string - 10th fret
2) 2nd string - 15th fret
3) 3rd string - 19th fret

5.
1) 4th string - 2nd fret
2) 5th string - 7th fret
3) 6th string - 12th fret

1) 1st string - open
2) 2nd string - 5th fret
3) 3rd string - 9th fret
4) 4th string - 14th fret
5) 5th string - 19th fret

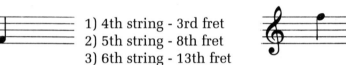
1) 1st string - 12th fret
2) 2nd string - 17th fret
3) 3rd string - 21st fret

6.
1) 4th string - 3rd fret
2) 5th string - 8th fret
3) 6th string - 13th fret

1) 1st string - 1st fret
2) 2nd string - 6th fret
3) 3rd string - 10th fret
4) 4th string - 15th fret
5) 5th string - 20th fret

1) 1st string - 13th fret
2) 2nd string - 18th fret

7.
1) 3rd string - open
2) 4th string - 5th fret
3) 5th string - 10th fret
4) 6th string - 15th fret

1) 1st string - 3rd fret
2) 2nd string - 8th fret
3) 3rd string - 12th fret
4) 4th string - 17th fret

1) 1st string - 15th fret
2) 2nd string - 20th fret

For sharp or flat notes just move one fret up or down

eg   G♯ 1st string - 4th fret   G♭ 1st string - 2nd fret
2nd string - 9th fret   2nd string - 7th fret
3rd string - 13th fret   3rd string - 11th fret

FINGERBOARD NOTE CHART

This chart will enable you to **find any note on any string** and is especially helpful when you first start using movable scale patterns and chord shapes, because it will answer the question "what key am I in?"

Strings	6th	5th	4th	3rd	2nd	1st	
open	E	A	D	G	B	E	open
Fret 1)	F	A♯/B♭	D♯/E♭	G♯/A♭	C	F	(1
2)	F♯/G♭	B	E	A	C♯/D♭	F♯/G♭	(2
3)	G	C	F	A♯/B♭	D	G	(3
4)	G♯/A♭	C♯/D♭	F♯/G♭	B	D♯/E♭	G♯/A♭	(4
5)	A	D	G	C	E	A	(5
6)	A♯/B♭	D♯/E♭	G♯/A♭	C♯/D♭	F	A♯/B♭	(6
7)	B	E	A	D	F♯/G♭	B	(7
8)	C	F	A♯/B♭	D♯/E♭	G	C	(8
9)	C♯/D♭	F♯/G♭	B	E	G♯/A♭	C♯/D♭	(9
10)	D	G	C	F	A	D	(10
11)	D♯/E♭	G♯/A♭	C♯/D♭	F♯/G♭	A♯/B♭	D♯/E♭	(11
12)	E	A	D	G	B	E	(12
13)	F	A♯/B♭	D♯/E♭	G♯/A♭	C	F	(13
14)	F♯/G♭	B	E	A	C♯/D♭	F♯/G♭	(14
15)	G	C	F	A♯/B♭	D	G	(15
16)	G♯/A♭	C♯/D♭	F♯/G♭	B	D♯/E♭	G♯/A♭	(16
17)	A	D	G	C	E	A	(17
18)	A♯/B♭	D♯/E♭	G♯/A♭	C♯/D♭	F	A♯/B♭	(18
19)	B	E	A	D	F♯/G♭	B	(19

The ability to read and write music can open up new worlds to the guitarist and it's a lot easier than you might think. Can you imagine how useful it can be to write down a tune you have just made up when there's no tape recorder available on which to "save" it? Oh yes and when later on its your first hit song wouldn't you be glad you didn't skip this part of the book!

Well whether you eventually write a hit song or not its worth while getting to know the rudiments of music.

Musical sounds are represented by the first seven letter of the alphabet. A.B.C.D.E.F.G. and are written as notes on a STAVE (or staff) consisting of FIVE LINES and FOUR SPACES.

(Numbered upwards)

Lines   Spaces

```
                    5 F
            4   D              4 E
        3  B                3 C
      2 G                 2 A
   1 E                  1 F
```

As you see the lines and spaces also have letter names and we can easily remember these by 1) The sentence Every Good Boy Deserves Favour for r the letters on the lines and 2) The spaces spell out the word F-A-C-E.

All guitar music is written in the TREBLE CLEF and this is it's sign.

The STAFF is divided into BARS by vertical lines called BARLINES

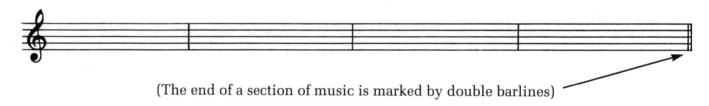

(The end of a section of music is marked by double barlines)

This is a note: ♪ it has three parts: The HEAD ●   STEM │ and FLAG ♪

Note may be placed:

In the stave   Above the stave   Below the stave

A note bears the name of the line or space it occupies on the stave eg.

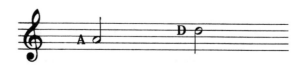

The location of a note in, above or below the stave indicates the pitch.

PITCH: The pitch simply means the highness or lowness of a tone.

TONE: A tone is a musical sound.

This is a WHOLE NOTE. **o**
(or Semibreve)
Hollow head: No stem.

This is a HALF NOTE.
(or Minim)
Hollow head: With stem.

This is a QUARTER NOTE.
(or Crotchet)
Solid head: With stem.

This is an EIGHTH NOTE.
(or Quaver)
Solid head: With stem and Flag

o = 4 Beats.
A Whole note
receives four
beats or counts.

= 2 Beats.
A Half note
receives two
beats or counts.

= 1 Beat.
A Quarter note
receives one
beat or count.

= 1/2 Beat.
A Eighth note
receives one half
beat or count.
(2 for 1 beat)

The relative note values in musical notation look like the examples below.

One (Semibreve)
Whole note.

is equal to
Two (Minims)
Half notes.

or,
Four (crotchets)
Quarter notes.

or,
Eight (Quavers)
Eighth notes.

In any piece of music there will be times when you don't actually play a note, it could be a very short time just a faction of a bar, or a long time lasting many bars. These periods of non playing are called funnily enough, RESTS.
So if you turn over the page quickly you'll have time for a rest.

R E S T S

Yes in music we also have RESTS. These are signs used to designate a period of silence and this period is always the same duration as the note to which it corresponds. The rest signs are shown below in the boxes.

A whole rest (Semibreve) hangs **down** from the line.	A Half rest (Minim) Lays **on** the line.
A Quarter rest (Crotchet)	An Eighth rest (Quaver)

NOTES AND THEIR CORRESPONDING RESTS

| WHOLE (SEMIBREVE) 4 COUNTS | HALF (MINIM) 2 COUNTS | QUARTER (CROTCHET) 1 COUNT | EIGHTH (QUAVER) 2 FOR 1 COUNT |

TIME SIGNATURES

The above are the common types of time signatures we'll be using in the book.

The TOP NUMBER 4 indicates **the number of beats per bar.**
The BOTTOM NUMBER 4 indicates **the type of note receiving one beat.**
  e.g. Quarter notes (crotchets) as in the above examples or Eight notes (Quavers) as in the following:

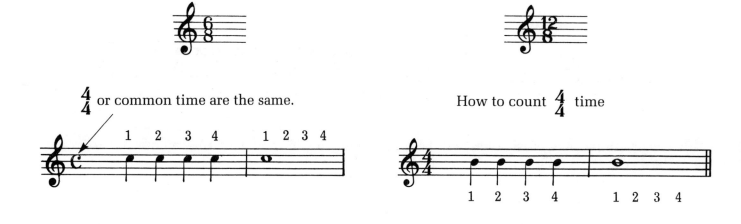

$\frac{4}{4}$ or common time are the same.

How to count $\frac{4}{4}$ time

We mentioned earlier that notes can not only be placed in the stave but also above or below it. This enables us to indicate notes of a higher or lower pitch than the compass of the stave. This is done by using short lines called LEDGER LINES.

They look like this:

The OPEN STRINGS of the guitar appear like this on the stave:

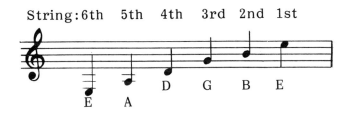

The usual range of the guitar written in the Treble Clef:

Electric guitars will go up to a C♯ above that high A and the air gets kinda thin. This is how the extra high notes look on the ledger lines. (Scary isn't it)

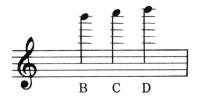

Not many beginners go up there and come back!
But relax, we won't be concerned about exploring that high on the fingerboard in this book.

Printed in Great Britain by Hobbs the Printers of Southampton 6/91